AI Concepts for Business Applications

AI Concepts for Business Applications

Applications

Nelson E. (Nick) Brestoff

BEP BUSINESS EXPERT PRESS

AI Concepts for Business Applications

Copyright © Business Expert Press, LLC, 2020.

First published in 2020 by
Business Expert Press, LLC
222 East 46th Street, New York, NY 10017
www.businessexpertpress.com

ISBN-13: 978-1-94999-168-0 (paperback)
ISBN-13: 978-1-94999-169-7 (e-book)

Business Expert Press Business Law and Corporate Risk Management Collection

Collection ISSN: 2333-6722 (print)
Collection ISSN: 2333-6730 (electronic)

Cover and interior design by Exeter Premedia Services Private Ltd., Chennai, India

First edition: 2020

10 9 8 7 6 5 4 3 2 1

Printed in the United States of America.

I dedicate this book to my wife Lois Ellen Montague Brestoff, J.D., to whom I've been happily married since 1975.

Abstract

The business world has been hearing about Artificial Intelligence (AI) and blockchain. AI was the superstar topic of conversations at the World Economic Forum in Davos, Switzerland this past January 2019.

Here, Nick Brestoff, a former attorney who now holds eight (8) patents for business applications that use AI and the breakthrough form of AI—"deep learning," provides his readers with a "no math" explanation of deep learning that's followed by numerous applications in a wide variety of contexts.

In this book, he opens the door to his journey of understanding and innovation, all in an effort to empower his readers to come up with business-relevant innovations of their own.

Keywords

Artificial Intelligence; blockchain; business applications; contracts; deep learning; early case assessment; e-discovery; entertainment; financial advantages; innovations; litigation; manufacturing; medical; patents; prevention; product defects; publishing; risk; tax planning

Contents

Acknowledgments

I thank all of the persons with whom I've worked since 2015, and especially the individuals who were hands-on in connection with the patents and implementing software, including Michael G. Becker, software developer F. Scott Barker, data scientist Jagannath Rajagopal; and patent attorneys Dan Cotman and Obi Iloputaife. I also thank Thomas D. Barton (Professor of Law at California Western School of Law) for reviewing, commenting on, and editing the manuscript, and attorney Sean LaRoque-Doherty for editing the Capstone chapter. I also thank Steve Bearman (Instructor, Computer Science, Peninsula College), Harpal Gill (VP, Global Alliances, SoftwareAG) and Patrick J. McKenna (law firm practice management consultant) for their helpful comments. I'm responsible for any and all errors.

All affiliations are for reference only, with no endorsements implied.

CHAPTER 1

Introduction

I wrote this book to explain the concepts of Artificial Intelligence (AI) in the form of *deep learning* to people in the business community who are *not* data scientists. You won't find equations here. This book is a no-math book.

As a preliminary matter, my subject matter expertise is law and litigation. I will often use the legal context because it's familiar to me, and I encourage you to take terms like "Commercial Tort Litigation," "litigation hold notices" and any other legal terms or phrases in stride. Please don't concern yourself with a lack of definition or further details. Just think of any of the "inside baseball" terms that I may mention as a placeholder for some term or phrase that may be familiar to *you* because of *your* expertise. Legal is my sand box.

My aim and hope is that this book will be important to you if you're a life-long learner and you want to use your subject-matter expertise to identify innovative applications of AI for your industry and in your areas of expertise.

My other goal is to help you appreciate what the AI *revolution* is all about, and why the phrase "deep learning" is what people are really talking about when they use the term AI.

I'm also writing this book because I think of myself as a lifelong learner. I learned enough of the conceptual framework for deep learning to come up with more than a handful of business applications *and* to obtain eight patents for them. If I can climb on top of deep learning, so can you.

But aside from remotely auditing a computer science course at Stanford (which was then called CS 224d and is CS 224n now), I'm *not* a trained data scientist.

However, long ago, I earned a B.S. degree in Engineering Systems at UCLA, and then an M.S. degree in Environmental Engineering

Science at the California Institute of Technology. But after graduating from Caltech, I went to the Gould School of Law at the University of Southern California. After earning a J.D. degree, I was a litigation specialist in California for both plaintiffs and defendants in both state and federal courts from 1975 to 2014.

Thus, while I'm not unfamiliar with technology, I didn't have professional experience with engineering or technology. But in 2015, I began my second childhood. That's the step that allowed me to become an inventor of software systems that make use of deep learning.

Briefly, here's what happened.

During much of 2015, I was writing a book with computer scientist W. H. (Bill) Inmon, the father of the data warehouse. The book, *Preventing Litigation: An Early Warning System to Get Big Value Out of Big Data*, was published in the Fall of 2015 by Business Expert Press, the same publisher of this book.

I stand by *Preventing Litigation*. It's earned a perfect five-star rating from readers and it was endorsed by one of the world's foremost thought leaders for the legal profession, Sir Richard Susskind. He allowed me to use this line on the back cover: "As a lawyer or client, if you prefer a fence at the top of a cliff to an ambulance at the bottom, this insightful book is essential reading."

However, while I was editing *Preventing Litigation*, and before it was published, I saw an article that spoke to me. The news was that venture capitalists were starting to take AI seriously and had started to back an ever-growing list of startups. I mentioned AI and deep learning only in passing, on pages 169–170, as a possible alternative to the technology that Bill Inmon, my co-author, had described in Chapters 10–14. After *Preventing Litigation* was published, I diverted from the technology Bill had laid out. I still had the same business application in mind, that is, a software system to help corporate counsel (i.e., in-house attorneys) see litigation *risks* in time to nip them in the bud. As attorney Dan Sanders put it recently in the context of risk management, the mission I had set up in *Preventing Litigation* was to create the software that would "protect tomorrow, today."[1]

When *Preventing Litigation* was published, I had been living in Sequim, Washington (on the Olympic Peninsula) for less than two years.

In order to meet new people, I volunteered to be a mentor to the students at Sequim High School who were working after school hours on a robot that would compete in a national competition. I was fortunate in that one of the other mentors was Michael G. Becker. Mike had been a software engineer during a 40-year career that took him from IBM to Microsoft. I mentioned deep learning to Mike one day and he told me that he had previously come across "neural networks," and so was interested. I knew where to find the data for training a deep learning model of specific types of litigation and the data we could use as a testbed.

As luck would have it, one of the startups in that article I mentioned on page 169 of *Preventing Litigation* was MetaMind. When I looked up the MetaMind website, I saw an open API ("application programming interface") by which MetaMind was making its system available to third parties like us. If we had the appropriate training data, we could train a neural network. If we had the appropriate test data, we could evaluate the model. It took us about four months to create a rudimentary proof of concept.

During much of that time, my understanding was that, due to the U.S. Supreme Court decision in *Alice Corp. v. CLS Bank International*,[2] the United States Patent and Trademark Office (USPTO) was going to turn down every patent application for a software system on the grounds that the system was simply a task that a computer could do, and so was patent *ineligible*.

But on June 27, 2016, the Federal Circuit Court of Appeals published its decision in *Bascom Global v. AT&T Mobility*.[3] In that decision, the Federal Circuit expressed the notion that practitioners had misread the *Alice* decision. There was a "step two" in the *Alice* decision, and it was that if an application for a patent set out a software system with an "inventive concept," a patent application for such a system might be granted. In his *Bascom Global* opinion, Judge Raymond Chen explained that the patent at issue had passed this "step two" test and explained why: "As is the case here," he wrote, "an inventive concept can be found in the non-conventional and non-generic arrangement of known, conventional pieces."[4]

The *Bascom Global* opinion was inspirational. I wrote a provisional application and, with the assistance of patent attorney Dan Cotman and his colleague, Obi Iloputaife, my provisional application was filed four days later, on July 1, 2016.

This first step was crucial. I knew that the "provisional" I had filed would become my Priority Date under the new "first to file" amendment to the patent laws, and I have been building on it ever since then. By the end of 2018, I have turned my inventive concepts into seven additional U.S. software system applications that have been accepted by the USPTO and issued as patents.

Later in this book, after I've set the stage for the concepts of deep learning as applied to text in the context of words, I'll be using portions of the text from those patents as examples.

That said, I'll reiterate my hope that this book will enable you to apply deep learning to your own areas of subject matter expertise. Please read this book with that thought in mind, so that you may apply deep learning to situations that are unfamiliar to me, but which are familiar to you.

And please keep in mind that the way I expect to enable *you* to learn—from examples—turns out to be the way deep learning enables *computers* to learn.

Note: For readers of the electronic version, the links in the Notes at the end of the book are live. Readers of the print version will have to copy them into a browser.

Notes

1. Dan Sanders, Risk and Business, in *Corporate Counsel-Digital*, at 42 (April 2019).
2. *Alice Corp. Pty. Ltd. v. CLS Bank International*, 573 U.S. 208, 134 S. Ct. 2347 (2014).
3. *Bascom Global Internet Servs., Inc. v. AT & T Mobility, LLC*, 827 F.3d 1341 (Fed. Cir. 2016).
4. Ibid. at p. 1350.

CHAPTER 2

The Prevention Motivation

As I've said, my first book for Business Expert Press was published in August of 2015 and was entitled *Preventing Litigation: An Early Warning System to Get Big Value Out of Big Data*. I didn't see the hint of AI and deep learning until I was nearly finished with the editing process.

Previously, I had learned to "follow the money." So, for example, I noted that, in 2014, Google had acquired DeepMind (for something like $650 million) and that MetaMind had been launched in December that same year with an $8 million investment by Marc Benioff, the founder, chairman and co-CEO of Salesforce and by Vinod Khosla, one of the founders of Sun Microsystems and a renowned Silicon Valley investor.

The "big picture" was that venture capital firms had invested $310 million in AI startups in 2014, a 20x increase from the $15 million that startups had attracted in 2010.

I could see an even bigger future for deep learning, and I said so in *Preventing Litigation*, on page 197. I wanted some of the sand on that beach, but I had no idea then that I would later create some of it.

After *Preventing Litigation* was published, I paid attention to MetaMind. I reached out to its founder, Richard Socher, who had received his Ph.D. from Stanford in 2014, and asked what I needed to address my litigation topic. He replied: "Labeled data." And, as I have mentioned, that was the only hint I needed because, having been a litigator and as I will explain, I knew where I could go for the "labeled data."

But besides the insights of where to go for the data and what I could do with it, I already knew from my research for *Preventing Litigation* that what I wanted to build was worth my time and trouble to build it. The business case involved a software system that would lead to *less* litigation. I was not interested in more efficient ways of managing or conducting litigation that had already been filed. I knew that litigation was expensive, and a drain on net profit. I believed that a technology to enable "less litigation" would be valuable.

The important point here, which doesn't have anything to do with deep learning, is that, in the first nine chapters of *Preventing Litigation*, I had constructed the business case for an early warning system that was predictive and preventive in nature. I knew in advance that there was a strong business case for avoiding litigation.

In early January of 2016, I attended a Deep Learning Summit in San Francisco. I had seen that Richard Socher was going to be a speaker. I was eager to get his reaction to the size of the problem I was addressing and to an early version of a User Interface (UI). Our conversation was brief but instructive. Dr. Socher was amazed by the size of the problem ($160 billion per year based on data for 2001–2010) and his reaction to the UI I showed him was "You have to build this."

Now let's fast-forward by three years, to January of 2019. On January 31, 2019, Brian Peccarelli, the Chief Operating Officer of Thomson Reuters, noted in a blog post about Davos 2019 that the *superstar* of the conference—the topic that nearly everyone was talking about—was not a celebrity or a public figure. It was AI. Mr. Peccarelli's take-away was "[a]t last, we're seeing this transformative technology beginning to unlock its true potential, and we're also seeing ways it can help address some of the biggest problems of society."[1]

I want to say something about AI, the acronym for Artificial Intelligence. AI is very broad term. As the term is used, it's often short-hand for one of the subcategories that's being discussed. Machine Learning is a subset of AI; Neural Networks are a subset of Machine Learning; and *Multi-Layer* Neural Networks are a subset of Neural Networks.

The shorthand for a Multi-layer Neural Network is deep learning.

Unfortunately, deep learning is often then erroneously referred to as AI.

Is it true that AI will change your future? Yes and no. My view is that deep learning is *already* shaping the future, and that it will *continue* to do so.

That makes the history of deep learning worth noting, but I'm not going to recount the history for you here. That's a look in the rear-view mirror, and not a way to look at (or invent) the many ways that deep learning will take us forward.

But you can search the Internet for "deep learning history" and find several links. One post I like is "A History of Deep Learning," by Andrew Fogg, dated May 30, 2018.[2] Here's another example: Dataversity's "A Brief History of Deep Learning," by Keith D. Foote, dated February 7, 2017.[3]

Why is deep learning such a force for now and into the foreseeable future? Because it's software that has enabled computers to "learn."

Notes

1. Peccarelli (2019).
2. Fogg (2018).
3. Foote (2017).

CHAPTER 3

Images

We live in two worlds. That is, our brains perceive the world in two ways. With our eyes, we see, and so one world involves images. With our ears, we hear language and later on learn to use our eyes to read the written word.

Let's take images first, where a form of deep learning called a Convolutional Neural Network (CNN) holds sway.[1]

For an overview of how computers can learn to process and "understand" images, look for two TED talk titles. The first title is *The Wonderful and Terrifying Implications of Computers That Can Learn* by Jeremy Howard (December 2014). Howard is a data scientist, the former president of Kaggle, and is currently the founder of Fast.ai. His TED talk is about 20 minutes and has been seen by over 2.4 million viewers.

The second title is *How We're Teaching Computers to Understand Pictures* by Fei-Fei Li (May 2015). Dr. Li is a Professor of Computer Science at Stanford University. She is currently the Co-Director of Stanford's Human-Centered AI Institute. Her TED talk is about 18 minutes. It's been viewed about 2.5 million times.

Now let me give you a starting "overview" of business applications of deep learning for images, starting with one way that Walmart and Amazon use this new power.

Just visualize the many aisles of products in a Walmart or any other retailer. Some portion of one or more shelves in every single aisle is empty. Customers have taken items off the shelves. There are gaps and they need attention, in part so that Walmart can measure demand and in part so that the shelves can be re-stocked. For human employees, that's a laborious and boring job: walk the aisles; make notes; walk back to "receiving;" find the items; then enter the notes in a spreadsheet; and walk back to the aisles that need additional product and put the items on the shelves where they belong.

Some of these tasks can be automated. Consider a robot body with wheels (or a track), one or more cameras, and a deep learning "brain." With deep learning, the robot (without being sentient and without understanding anything) learns the pattern of the store; where certain items are placed for sale; and where the same items can be found in "receiving."

On October 17, 2017, Walmart announced that it was beginning to use shelf-scanning robots to audit 50 of its stores. The robots are tracking inventory, prices, and misplaced items. Walmart wants to save its human employees from tasks that are repeatable, predictable, and manual, so (currently) these "bots" don't have arms for re-stocking. Indeed, Walmart asserted in its 2017 announcement that no employees would lose their jobs.[2]

The trials in 2018 went well. On April 9, 2019, Walmart announced that "Automated Assistants" would help employees "work smarter." In a post, Elizabeth Walker, of Walmart Corporate Affairs, wrote that Walmart was sold on robots. "Every hero needs a sidekick," she wrote, "and some of the best have been automated. Think R2D2, Optimus Prime and Robby from *Lost in Space.* Just like Will Robinson and Luke Skywalker, having the right kind of support helps our associates succeed at their jobs." She went on to describe "new technologies" that would minimize the time an employee might spend "cleaning floors" or "checking inventory on a shelf," and instead let them spend more time serving customers on the sales floor. What's coming? 1,500 new autonomous floor cleaners, aka Auto-C; 300 additional shelf scanners, aka Auto-S, 1,200 more FAST Unloaders, and 900 new Pickup Towers.[3]

As a second example, consider Amazon. Amazon is not a "big box" retailer in the same sense as Walmart. Amazon is the foremost example of an e-commerce retailer. Amazon relies on shipping product from its plethora of warehouses. In the same article announcing that Walmart was beginning to use shelf-scanning robots, the author noted that Amazon was already using more than forty-five *thousand* (45,000) "bots" in its warehouses.

If you think these examples are confined to the United States, think again: deep learning is having an impact worldwide. I've already mentioned Davos. It's the annual meeting place of the World Economic Forum. If AI is what everyone at Davos 2019 was talking about, then some of the attendees are from countries where English is *not* the native language.

Are examples hard to find? No. Here's one. On May 4, 2016, an Israeli company, eyeSight Technologies, announced a $20 million investment by a Chinese conglomerate, Kuang-Chi, to finance eyeSight's embedded computer vision and deep learning technologies to a variety of sectors, such as the Internet of Things (IoT), robotics, and automotive.[4]

Fast forward to March 12, 2019, when Eyesight Technologies announced that it had signed a "strategic cooperation agreement" with Chinese Tier 1 automotive vendor Hefei Zhixin Automotive Technology (HZAT), whose relationships include major China OEM brands including JAC Motors and bus manufacturer Anhui Ankai Automobile Co. Eyesight's Drive Sense monitoring system "watches a driver's eyes, pupils, head and gaze to determine if the driver is paying attention to the road or is drowsy or distracted." If warranted, the system will take over the vehicle "to prevent accidents."[5]

Let's stick with images. AI is frequently associated with autonomous vehicles such as cars on the road or drones in the air. But let's come back to the United States, where two car companies come to mind: Tesla and Waymo.

Tesla has self-driving capabilities via its Autopilot system. Autopilot is Tesla's advanced assisted driving program with features like Autosteer, Autopark, and Traffic-Aware Cruise Control (TACC). Currently, with over 250,000 "cars" on the road, Tesla may have deployed the largest fleet of robots in the world, and for the reason that the "cars" are regularly driven in autonomous mode.

Notice that I said autonomous *mode.* Currently, Tesla's cars are not driverless.

But that day may come. On October 15, 2018, Tesla's Autopilot's v9 was described as having an ability to recognize roadside structures and a deep learning system with far larger processing capability than in previous versions.[6] More specifically and in the same article, Elon Musk, Tesla's founder and CEO, replied in a Tweet that the "V9.0 vs. V8.1 is more like a ~400 percent increase in useful ops/sec due to enabling integrated GPU and better use of discrete GPU." @elonmusk on October 16, 2018. (A GPU stands for a graphics processing unit or "graphics card.")

For the current articles about Tesla's Autopilot, go to Electrek.co.[7] For example, that is as of late May 2019, you can watch a Tesla, using Autopilot, react to a stop sign and make a right turn.[8]

The project for that ability was initiated and accomplished in only about two years. You may already know that, with images, the amount of training data a deep learning system needs to be accurate is enormous. Since Tesla didn't already have data centers with millions of miles of visuals, it sold a lot of early models and then asked its customers for help. When Autopilot 2.0 was released in May of 2017, Tesla asked its car owners *in advance* for permission to collect data from its external cameras "to learn how to recognize things like lane lines, street signs, and traffic light positions," assuring them for the sake of privacy that its external cameras were not linked to vehicle identification numbers.

Thus, using Wi-Fi, Tesla began getting a huge influx of image data, and the data was coming from the Model S cars it had sold and which were already on the road.[9]

I'm reminded of the 1986 movie, *Short Circuit*, where a robot named "Johnny 5" goes off the research reservation because it had a craving for "input."[10] Tesla reminds me of the Lab that lost track of Johnny 5, except that Tesla didn't lose track of its Model S cars and started with 50,000 of them. Now Autopilot has moved from v2.0 to v9 and has had a lot of "input."

So Tesla is a mobile robot and can take us to places we've never visited. It's just a look-see, but for a treat, click on this September 25, 2018 link to watch a Tesla drive in Paris through the "eyes" of Autopilot.[11]

Wow. I have to pause here, because an AI business application just occurred to me. If Tesla's Autopilot can take us on a drive through Paris, it can take viewers on a drive through other places of interest. But now think about recording "tours" through other cities, national parks, or various vacation destinations. Where might such tours be displayed? On a website? Could be. How about on small screens during travel by air? Yes, that's another potential application. And how about a television "travel" channel or YouTube channel? Or in a home on a screen attached to a workout treadmill? If I could go places (virtually) on a treadmill, I might actually buy one.

Tesla may be an energy company (think batteries) and an automaker, but it also has a software product.

Waymo, on the other hand, was known initially as the Google Self-Driving Car Project, which Google started in 2009. The Self-Driving Car Project is now independent of Google and is known as Waymo.[12]

As of March 20, 2019, Waymo's website reports putting its autonomous vehicles through a lot: 10 million miles on public road and 7 *billion* miles in simulation. And, of course, with deep learning and every mile driven, Waymo is correct to assert that "we never stop learning." If you visit the Waymo website, you'll see the "brain" of the vehicle has answers to "Where am I?" "What's around me?" "What will happen next?" and "What should I do?"

Waymo answers the last question by asserting: "Based on all this information, our software determines the exact trajectory, speed, lane, and steering maneuvers needed to progress along this route safely."[13] You can also watch the Waymo 360-degree Experience: A Fully Self-Driving Journey.

Hmm. I had wondered about the source of Waymo's 7 billion miles of *simulation*; that is, until I remembered Street View. Remember Street View? Launched in 2007 by Google Maps, Google put out fleets of vehicles to drive the streets in one location after another. Their cars were equipped with video cameras and other sensors that were intended to enable users to "virtually explore the world."[14]

Currently, while Google's fleets have already covered much of the world, its fleets are still out there, and going new places all the time. And Google lets you discover where the fleets are going next and when.[15]

Although I'm not certain of this, my guess is that Waymo had a simulation "head start" by way of access to the Street View videos.

But to better understand autonomous vehicles, let's think the system through. What's the input? The input consists of images (in pixels) from cameras and various sensors, for example, infrared and lidar, which is short for "light detection and ranging."[16] What's the output? It's *mechanical*. The cars are still riding along on wheels and they are controlled by brakes, the gas pedal, and the steering wheel. What's in-between the input and output? It's a deep learning "brain," and it consists of software.

Now, with these examples in mind, let's consider some very different applications. These examples will help you understand the versatility of deep learning in the context of images. As a prelude, I remind you that our world is visual by *our* very nature. In fact, our eyes are the one and only part of our human biological system that is connected directly to our brains. Look around: applications are *everywhere*.

Let's take ag-tech first. Consider a drone with cameras, deep learning software, and a sprayer. What's the application? It's a weed or insect killer. The drone flies up and down the long and seemingly unending rows of crops that have been planted. The software has been trained to identify, on the one hand, what the farmer wants to grow, and, on the other hand, the weeds and/or insects the farmer knows are threats to his or her harvest. The deep learning software is trained to spray the weed-killer or insecticide where the spray will do the most good, and to do so *without hitting the crops.*

Don't believe me? See what Blue River Technology (acquired by John Deere in 2017) has already implemented with "lettuce bot" and "See and Spray" applications.[17]

Or how about a drone that helps farmers "see" where to apply fertilizers or add more irrigation? Yep, in a research paper, that's been envisioned too.[18]

Now what about disasters? How would you envision a deep learning application in that context? Well, how about right *after* a disaster, which could be an earthquake, flood, forest fire, or something else? The first responders who are unfamiliar with the locale should be deployed where they can do the most good, right? That mission calls for priorities. Which portions of the infrastructure (bridges, buildings, telephone and electrical poles) are too damaged to warrant immediate attention? What portions are not damaged and need no attention? And, more to the point, what portions are only slightly damaged and can be returned to service if only the appropriate responders and resources were immediately devoted to the task?

That's triage, a term that's more frequently associated with battlefield medicine but which applies just as well to what some of the first responders should be doing with respect to infrastructure, when they're responding to a disaster.

But who's going to tell them where to go? Well, it's a drone again, with a camera, and with software that can identify what's been damaged *and to what extent.* For this inventive application, watch the video about Ocean IT's ioView Computer Vision for Rapid Damage Assessment. With this application, "recovery crews can map, evaluate, tag, and allocate repair resources and personnel to specific areas far more quickly than ever before."[19]

And then there's medicine itself. Think about X-rays and MRIs. There's actually a lot of "visual" in medicine. There are numerous applications here, and I'll tell you about two of them. The first application is a deep learning system to accurately assess whether indications of metastatic breast cancer are present or not. Google reported a system to do this only a few months ago, on October 12, 2018. The system is called LYNA, a shorthand for Lymph Node Assistant. In two datasets, LYNA was able to distinguish a slide with metastatic cancer from a slide where the cancer was not present. Better still, "LYNA was able to accurately pinpoint the location of both cancers and other suspicious regions within each slide, some of which were too small to be consistently detected by pathologists. As such we reasoned that one potential benefit of LYNA would be to highlight these areas of concern for pathologists to review and determine the final diagnosis."[20]

And here's another example of another non-U.S. collaboration that was recently reported (December 20, 2018) in the Journal of the American Medical Association (JAMA) for Ophthalmology. The study was carried out by medical research scientists at the Centre for Eye Research in Australia and the State Key Laboratory of Ophthalmology in China.

Here, the problem was one familiar to data scientists. Deep learning models may appear to be accurate but, as this study puts it, "the rationale for the outputs generated by these systems is inscrutable to clinicians. A visualization tool is needed …"

This study not only validated the deep learning models for retinal images (using CNNs), but also it verified the reliability of a visualization method so "that [the findings] may promote clinical adoption of these models." The work resulted in an automated grading system based on photographs.

I'll report the Findings as they were stated:

In this cross-sectional study, lesions typically observed in cases of referable diabetic retinopathy (exudate, hemorrhage, or vessel abnormality) were identified as the most important prognostic regions in 96 of 100 true-positive diabetic retinopathy cases. All 100 glaucomatous optic neuropathy cases displayed heat map visualization within traditional disease regions.

The Conclusions (where DLA means "deep learning algorithm" and DR refers to "diabetic retinopathy") were: "This artificial intelligence-based

DLA can be used with high accuracy in the detection of vision-threatening referable DR in retinal images. This technology offers potential to increase the efficiency and accessibility of DR screening programs."[21]

To sum up: now you know that the version of deep learning which consists of CNNs can learn from *visual* examples in a wide variety of contexts.

Notes

1. "Convolutional Neural Network" (2019).
2. Vincent (2017).
3. Walker (2019).
4. "Chinese Technology Conglomerate Kuang Chi to invest $20 Million in EyeSight Technologies, a Leader in Embedded Computer Vision" (2017).
5. "Eyesight Technologies closes new China Auto Deal with Hefei Zhixin Automotive" (2019).
6. Lambert (2018).
7. Lambert (2019).
8. Lambert (2019).
9. Lambert (2017).
10. "Short Circuit" (2019).
11. Lambert (2018).
12. "We're building the World's Most Experienced Driver" (2019).
13. "Technology" (2019).
14. "What is Street View" (2019).
15. "Sources of Photography" (2019).
16. NOAA (National Oceanic and Atmospheric Administration) (2012).
17. "Optimize Every Plant" (2019).
18. "AI and Drones Help Farmers Detect Crop Needs" (2018).
19. "IO View is a Computer vision AI for Rapid Damage Assessment Named After the Native Hawaiian Hawk" (2019).
20. Stumpe and Mermel (2018).
21. Keel, Wu, Lee, Scheetz, and He (2018).

CHAPTER 4

Words

Chapter 3 was about images. I had been a lawyer and members of my family will tell you that I'm not a visual person. I like numbers but I swim in words. And for words, a different form of deep learning is dominant: a Recurrent Neural Network (RNN). And RNNs also learn from examples. But, in order to "understand" a specific topic, the examples must come from (and be related to) that topic.

The bottom line of RNNs is that the training data comes from examples that are labeled (the word Richard Socher used), or categorized or classified.[1]

Initially, when I found it in 2015, I was impressed with a YouTube presentation in November of 2012, in which Rick Rashid, then the head of Microsoft Research was speaking to a Chinese audience. He spoke in English. On the left side of a split screen, his words appeared on a crawler (at the bottom) in English. On the right side, his words appeared in Chinese characters.

But the "wow" moment was when the Chinese characters were turned into Chinese *speech* that the Chinese audience could and did understand. The audience broke into spontaneous applause and, it's fair to say, the taciturn Chinese are not known for that sort of reaction. The YouTube video runs just over nine minutes, and the description states, "[t]he breakthrough is patterned after deep neural networks and significantly reduces errors in spoken as well as written translation."[2]

So deep learning was evident every step of the way. Rashid's voice was an audio signal. Deep learning pattern-matched the sounds of his words to the text on the crawler. Then deep learning pattern-matched Rashid's words to the Chinese characters that appeared in the crawler on the right side of the split. And for the last step, the characters were pattern-matched to the sounds a voice would make if Rashid's voice was speaking Chinese.

Once I saw that video (I recommend it), I knew then that the door was going to open for deep learning as applied to text.

Now, more than six years on, if you go to the Skype website, you'll see that the *voice* translator can handle conversations in real time in 10 languages, including English, Spanish, French, German, Chinese (Mandarin), Italian, Portuguese (Brazilian), Arabic, and Russian; and that the *text* translator is available for more than 60 languages for "clear, seamless instant messaging."[3]

Now you know something about deep learning. It's CNNs for images and RNNs for text. And you know that applications are popping up with rapidity in both contexts.

So, before going on to applications in the legal space (contracts, litigation), I'd like to pull the curtain back on two other linchpin concepts. The first concept is the linguistics theory that describes, in only a few words, how we communicate with each other using words. The second concept is how words can be turned into number strings (called vectors) so that a computer can process them.

Let's take a linguistic theory first. There is a well-respected theory due to the late linguist J. R. Firth. It's simple. He taught that "You shall know a word by the company it keeps."[4] What that single sentence means is that *context* is the key to understanding the way we use words to communicate with each other.

This theory also explains why a search through text-based data using key words is vulnerable to error. With a key word, we're using a needle to search through a haystack and the problem is that the key word has been taken out of context. One key word within "x" words of another key word is better, but is still out of range (and out of context) as to the other adjacent words. A *list* of key words is no better. A list offers almost no context because the list carries no information about how each word is related to the other words on the list or in any other word in the data to be searched. Key words are a leaky boat.

Aside from key words, there is another technique called Latent Semantic Analysis (or Indexing),[5] where Latent means "hidden" and Semantic means "meaning." If I have a digital stack of documents (a "corpus"), and I'm looking for a document that uses the word "gun," I *will* find a document with the word "gun" in it. But I will not find a document that's potentially highly relevant but does not contain the word "gun" because it only uses the word "firearm."

The reason the LSA approach was an advance is that it makes use of the *co-occurrence* of other words. To explain, I'll continue with the same "gun" and "firearm" documents. With LSA, I might use the key word "gun," and find a document with "gun" in it. And I might *also* find a document containing the word "firearm" and which does not contain the word "gun," but I'll find the "firearm" document *if*, for example, the word "bullet" *co-occurs* in both documents.

LSA was an improvement, but the technique does not keep each word in context. If we want to train a deep learning model, so that it learns a pattern of discourse, we have to turn each word into a number string so that a computer can process it. The process of converting words in a document to a group of number strings (a vector "space"), so that a computer can process the strings (vectors), is called a "word embedding."

That process was invented in 2013 when Tomas Mikolov and others at Google invented a technique called word2vec. The purpose of word2vec is to turn words into number strings (vectors). It works to cluster documents that are related to each other, because the documents are in the same category or classification, and the words in one document are associated with the other words in other documents *in the same category*.

For example, the words in a lawsuit describing the factual basis for employment discrimination are not likely to match up well with the factual allegations in an antitrust case.

With enough examples, a label, classification, or category may be sufficiently well defined for pattern-matching that's highly accurate.

But another way to think of this process would be more granular, where the strings are based on how each word in a document is related to the few words before and after it.

Suppose you could draw a rectangle around five words in sequence.[6] See Figure. 4.1. For each rectangle, the middle word is the focus. It gets a number string. But then, looking back two words and their number strings, the middle word (now a number string) is augmented *by them*. And then, looking forward, the middle word is augmented in the same way by the number strings of the two words that *follow it*.

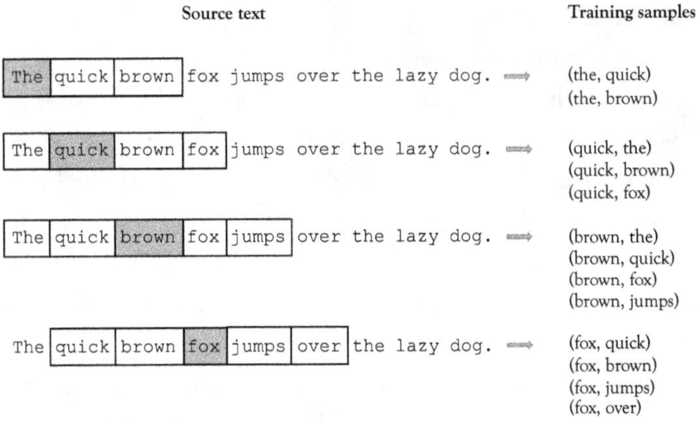

Source text   Training samples

| The | quick | brown | fox jumps over the lazy dog. ⟹ | (the, quick) |
| | | | | (the, brown) |

The quick brown fox jumps over the lazy dog. ⟹   (quick, the)
(quick, brown)
(quick, fox)

The quick brown fox jumps over the lazy dog. ⟹   (brown, the)
(brown, quick)
(brown, fox)
(brown, jumps)

The quick brown fox jumps over the lazy dog. ⟹   (fox, quick)
(fox, brown)
(fox, jumps)
(fox, over)

Figure 4.1 "You shall know a word by the company it keeps"—J. R. Firth

See? The number string (vector) for the middle word now has nuance, having been augmented by the vectors of the two words before *and* after them. The middle word has neighbors and they and the number strings for it are in context; and if they're in the same classification of documents, the words are related in that way too.

But now move the rectangle (the "window") one word to the right, and we're looking at a new middle word. Now we're looking at the two words before and after that new middle word.

In this way, you can see that *if* the middle word is "dog," this approach will keep the word in context. If I take any word by itself, and so take it out of context, I won't get very far.

Here's how I get that point across to an audience. I ask them this: If I say the word "dog," what topic comes to your mind? One common response is "pet," and I say no. Then I hear "German Shepard," or some other breed, and again I say no. Invariably, someone then goes against the grain, and says the opposite, as in "cat." And again I say no.

To make the point, I say that I was thinking about a different context, as in a *food*, and as in "hot dog."

So far, no one's been able to read my mind. Context matters, but what does that mean? It means that when the context is established first by a label, category, or classification, the words in that context are not likely to jump from one meaning to another. If the context of a word can be also defined by the words before and after it, then that approach may be better still.

So take the word "Ford," modified by the word before it. Clearly, "Gerald Ford" means someone other than "Henry Ford." The context is a President, not an innovative industrialist. How about changing the word that follows? The context changes. For example, the context for the phrase "Ford Motor" is about a company that makes automobiles. That context is close to but is yet different from "Ford Mustang," a type of automobile that the company makes. Moreover, the two words, "Ford a" is meaningless, but "ford a river" means to cross a river and is something else entirely.[7]

So, if the examples of a classification of documents can be collected in such a way that the words in each document in the classification can be kept in context, then the documents, with all of the words in them, can be turned into number strings typical of the classification. This sort of training data to create a deep learning model is called "supervised learning." One document won't do. Many documents "as examples" are needed.

But to train a deep learning model for a specific classification of text, we may only need tens or hundreds or thousands of documents, and nothing like the amount of data that is needed for images, as when Waymo was initially trained with seven billion miles of simulation.

In 2014, word2vec was extended to Global Vectors for Word Representation, or GloVe.[8] GloVe is an *unsupervised* learning algorithm [i.e., no classification is needed] for obtaining vector representations of words. In a sense, given enough words, GloVe learns English. The authors of the GloVe paper were Jeffrey Pennington, Richard Socher (remember him?), and Christopher Manning, who is a well-known Computer Science professor at Stanford.

Thankfully, GloVe is both open-source (available to the public at no charge) and, as I write, is still the state-of-the-art.

Let's summarize the story so far. For text, a deep learning model for a classification will need examples of documents in that classification; and all of the words must be kept in context, and yet nevertheless be converted to numbers that a computer can process.

You don't need to understand the details. You only need to know that this *translation* from the way *we* understand words (in context) to the way a *computer* can create a "model" of the number strings is a "word embedding."

Once you've compiled enough examples for a word-based model, it's a pattern. And *then* a computer can use GloVe again to process words it's *never seen before.* The computer can also compare those vectors to the model's vectors and report back as to whether any of the previously unseen words match up with the model *and to what degree.*

That's pattern-matching. Pattern-matching is a mapping from A to B. B is the deep learning model that's been trained by feeding in data consisting of labeled examples. A is the data the model's never seen before. Does A match up with B?

My analogy for this pattern-matching is a visualization: an archery target, but a target with no concentric circles. It's just a blank. Instead of standing back and shooting arrows at it, and hoping to get close to the center and achieve a high score, we walk right up to the target, with our exemplary (training) arrows in hand, and we stuff them into the center. See Figure 4.2. Because the arrows are exemplary of the specific category of interest to us, we have *defined* for the target what *we* would call a bullseye.

To create a binary classifier (yes and no; ones and zeros), we could complete this analogy by putting thumbtacks (meaning "off the mark" or "negatives") all around where the arrows (the "positives") were clustered.

Could a model be imprecise? Yes. If there are arrows among the thumbtacks or thumbtacks among the arrows, the model will be imprecise. But if the arrows are tightly clustered, with no thumbtacks, while the

Figure 4.2 The arrows analogy. Thumbtacks not shown

Document level t-SNE embeddings

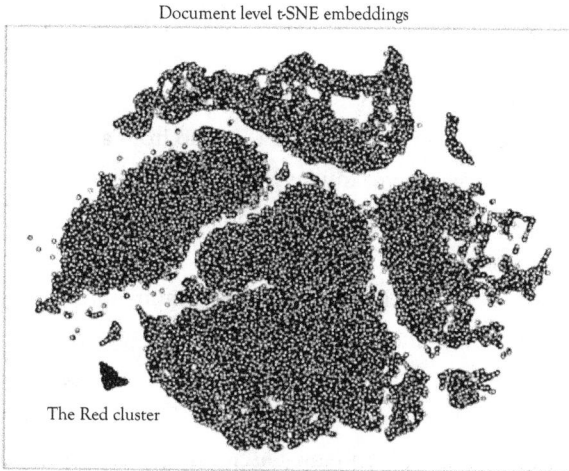

The Red cluster

Figure 4.3 The Red cluster (consisting only of arrows, with no thumbtacks) is positive training data. The White cluster (consisting only of thumbtacks, with no arrows) is negative training data. Result: A strong binary classifier. Actual training data

rest of the target has only thumbtacks and no arrows, then we have a clear boundary for decision making. See Figure 4.3.

Now, let's step back and shoot darts at the target. By "darts" I mean the *test* data, the data the model has never seen before. Do any of the darts come close to or hit the area defined by the arrows as the bullseye? If so, those darts can be scored, and report to us that they matched up with the bullseye (the arrows). Better still, the scores will indicate whether the darts are closer to the center of the arrows (strong match) or closer to the edge of the arrows (weak match). If the darts are among the thumbtacks, they match up with the negative set and are not related to the model. If the darts match up with the thumbtacks, they won't score at all, and we won't want to know about them. The system will let them pass. If they match up with the arrows, we have ourselves a filter that's telling us which of the results are "related" to the model and to what degree.

There's one more step. It's up to a human to assess whether a dart that matches up and so is "related" to the classification is a True Positive or a False Positive.

And now you know why some of us refer to AI as a tool for putting computers to *our* service. And when we think of computers in that spirit,

AI doesn't mean Artificial Intelligence. AI means Augmented *Human* Intelligence.

Now, let's go back in time, maybe a hundred years ago, when a new technology called the automobile was a step up from a bicycle. Of course, most people in that era were familiar with horses and there were few if any roads. But the manufacturers of automobiles were willing to prove their point by racing against the horses.

Well, now I'll ask you to consider an AI v. human contest, but with a twist: a contest for accuracy *and* speed.

On February 26, 2018, legal tech startup, LawGeex, announced the results of an AI v. Lawyers competition. The competition involved issue-spotting in five standard Non-Disclosure Agreements (NDAs). The competitors were LawGeex's AI-based system (which uses deep learning) and 20 U.S-trained and very experienced lawyers. The competition was overseen by an independent consultant and lawyer, and involved input from academics, data scientists, and legal and machine-learning experts.

Here's the bottom line (quoting from the Study report): LawGeex "achieved an average **94 percent accuracy rate**, ahead of the lawyers who achieved **an average rate of 85 percent**." (Boldface in the original.)

But here's the stunner: It took the lawyers an average of *92 minutes* to review all five NDAs, while the LawGeex AI-based system reviewed all five NDAs in only *26 seconds.*[9]

Now recall that I had "discovered" deep learning during the last four months of 2015. It wasn't until March 5–6, 2018, in Los Angeles, California, that I realized another set of connections.

At the time, I was sitting in a conference room in the Beverly Hilton Hotel. I was there to be a co-facilitator at the first "Legal Ops" Institute of Today's General Counsel, an organization where corporate ("in-house") counsel meet to address issues and share information with each other. As a former California litigator and known as someone familiar with deep learning, I was there as a resource.

My realization consisted of an insight that came to me just before it was my turn to lead the conversation. Just before I spoke, I realized that, when asked about what AI does, attorneys were befuddled. Sure enough, when I did speak, I couldn't generate a viable conversation among the attorneys around the table.

So I tried yet another analogy. As I've shown, one task a deep learning model does with GloVe and RNNs, and does well with text, is pattern-matching. That is, the model learns the pattern of facts as alleged in a specific classification or type of lawsuits—for example, breach of contract, employment discrimination, or fraud—which, in turn, enables a computer to process and score text in the form of e-mails that were not in the training data, and to output which of them are "related" to the type of litigation, and to what degree.

Here's the connection I tried to make for the attorneys. I asked them to recall what they learned to do in law school, which is to read lots of published court opinions on a specific topic, say in a class about contracts. Without realizing it, they were learning *precedents* of law that were established by key facts in those opinions.

Precedents are previous decisions, as handed down by previous decision makers who faced a similar situation. Take a course in the law of contracts and you'll learn about the appellate precedents or statutes that have been handed down in laws passed by a legislature, in regulations crafted by regulatory authorities, or in opinions by jurists.

But of course, after graduating, passing the Bar Exam, and getting sworn in, every litigator gets to meet his or her first client. And that person either wants to bring a lawsuit or has been sued and needs a defense. After the introductions, the inevitable first questions are easy for anyone to imagine: It's as simple as "What brings you here? Please tell me what's happened."

And you can readily imagine the rest of that first conversation. But here's what the lawyer's thinking "Ah, this is a family law matter." Or it's "Oh, I see where this is going. It's a fraud case."

Or it's some other category. But whatever the category, that's just the classification or, as Richard Socher would say, the label. But along with that, one or two *precedents* may come to mind. Or the facts may not ring any bells? Do these facts match up with an already-decided lawsuit that's now in the books? Do the facts being recounting add up to a strong case for or against him or her?

And these initial musings are what legal research is all about: Look up the precedents before you give any advice or even agree to be involved.

See the connection? Remember, we're in a digital era and have only recently discovered that we can build software that enables computers to learn. And one way they learn, with words, is very similar to the way attorneys have been trained to think: match new fact patterns against the precedents of how similar factual situations have been assessed in the past.

The stories that bring litigants into court are human stories. Juries can listen to the facts and get the story from the documents admitted into evidence and the testimony of the witnesses. The members of the jury listen to the arguments and vote.

But what if there's just too much data for us to ingest and assess? Could any attorney working in a corporate legal department read the e-mails from yesterday's batch and find the few e-mails that might be seen as "smoking guns" in some future lawsuit? No. There are too many e-mails.

Can deep learning help us then?

Yes. That's the power of computers. Digital memories have capacities far larger than our own, and computers can process data at speeds that far surpass the speed of our abilities to process that much information. Remember the LawGeex result: the attorneys needed 92 minutes while the computer needed only 26 seconds.

That said, let me switch to the next level up from the observation that precedents, when collected, become patterns. The next realization is that, from patterns, *predictions* can be reliably made.

That realization didn't originate with me and in fact came from an unexpected source. Just before a 2018 U.S. Chamber of Commerce conference in Seattle, I had been on a plane going to the Summit on Law and Innovation at Vanderbilt Law School in Nashville. The flight from Seattle to Nashville finally afforded me the time to read a book. On the plane going back to Seattle, I re-read it.

What an eye-opener. The book is *Prediction Machines*, subtitled, *The Simple Economics of Artificial Intelligence*, written by Professors Ajay Agarwal, Joshua Gans, and Avi Goldfarb, all three of whom are economists and Professors at the University of Toronto's Rotman School of Management.[10]

These three academics also had binocular vision. Besides their academic focus, they had founded the Creative Destruction Lab (CDL), a seed-stage program to support science-based startups. As they put it, on page 2 of their book, CDL's most exciting ventures were AI-enabled companies and, as of September 2017, the CDL had (for the third year in a row) interfaced with the largest cohort of AI startups of any program on the planet.

From that advantaged perch, the authors launched their book with their "first key insight," which is that "the new wave of artificial intelligence does not actually bring us intelligence but instead a critical component of intelligence—*prediction*." (Italics in the original.)

And they were only on page 2.

In Chapter 2 of *Prediction Machines*, there was a second major insight. Prediction, they say, is "the process of filling in missing information." Cheaper predictions will mean more predictions because, they say, when the cost of something valuable falls, there will be more of it.

That puts us on the road to disruption. Predictions are being used to solve traditional problems now, but they will be used to solve nontraditional problems in the future. And then something else happens: the value of other things, which they and other economists call "complements," increases. As an example, they write that if the cost of coffee goes down, and we drink more of it, the demand for and value of sweeteners and sugar goes up. When autonomous vehicles begin making highly accurate and reliable predictions, the value of the sensors that capture the data representing the oncoming surroundings will go up.

In fact, they write, "Some AIs will affect the economics of a business so dramatically that they will no longer be used to simply enhance productivity in executing against the strategy; they will change the strategy itself." [11]

Now what do they mean by that? They mean that, for Amazon, the current strategy is to enable "shop, then ship." But they also mean that if the processes of delivery and handling returns are so accurately predicted that their respective costs go down significantly, then, perhaps with regional warehouses, a new model might emerge: "ship, then shop."

And that's just the end of *Chapter* 2.

By the time they reach the end of their book, the authors are explaining why the likes of the AI-enabled tech companies—Google and Microsoft—have already seen the future and that, having seen it, they have transformed their companies (in 2017) from "mobile-first" to "AI-first."

In Chapter 17, they're explaining that such a shift "means compromising on other goals such as maximizing revenue, user numbers, or user experience."

Why? What's the explanation for *that* assertion? Here it is, on p. 194:

AI can lead to disruption because incumbent firms often have weaker economic incentives than startups to adopt the technology. AI-enabled products are often inferior at first because it takes time to train a prediction machine to perform as well as a hard-coded device that follows human instructions rather than learning on its own. However, once deployed, an AI can continue to learn and improve, leaving its unintelligent competitors' products behind.[12]

Or, as Jeremy Howard put it, we now live in an era when computers can learn. Now you know that it's the deep learning software that learns, and that it's trained in a way that we learn: from examples. And with additional examples, they keep learning.

And *that's* the reason why AI deserves close attention by everyone who's running a business or wants to lead one.

The second reason is that AI researchers keep improving the tools. I've mentioned word2vec (2013) and GloVe (2014) as word embedding tools for converting words to number strings. As of 2018, we now have ELMo and BERT to consider as well.

For example, consider a contrived sentence that contains the same word three times but for three different meanings: "*He went to the prison cell with his cell phone to extract blood cell samples from inmates.*"

The labels have jumped from prison to phones to blood. Yikes.

Well, ELMo and BERT are different from word2vec and GloVe in that they can generate *different* word embeddings for the same word even when that word has three different meanings *in the same sentence.*[13] How long will it take for ELMo and BERT to go from academia to state-of-the-art? My guess is "not long."

Notes

1. Rouse (2018).
2. "Speech Recognition Breakthrough for the Spoken, Translated Word" (2012).
3. Microsoft Speech Translator (2019).
4. Church (2007).
5. "Latent semantic analysis" (2019).
6. McCormick (2019).
7. Radford (2009).
8. Pennington, Socher, and Manning (2014).
9. "AI vs. Lawyers: The Ultimate Showdown" (2018).
10. Agrawal, Gans, and Goldfarb (2018).
11. Ibid.
12. Ibid.
13. Rajasekharan (2019).

CHAPTER 5

The 4th Revolution

Let's step back and consider the history we've lived and attempt to recognize where we've been. Many observers will tell us that we're in a 4th Revolution, and I'm going to drop "Industrial" when describing the one we're in now.

I'll recount the previous Revolutions to be clear: The Industrial Revolution (Revolution No. 1) featured water, waterwheels, and steam power.

Industrial Revolution No. 2 featured electricity, which *then* changed *everything*. Revolution No. 3 relied on computers for automation and production at scale.

Today's Revolution No. 4 is the digital (or information) era that relies on software and has finally found an inflection point, by which I mean the "elbow" of an exponential curve. Deep learning may be in its infancy but it's been noticed. For example, on September 26, 2016, *Fortune* published an article by Roger Parloff entitled *Why Deep Learning Is Suddenly Changing Your Life.*[1]

Now I'll introduce Professor Andrew Ng. He's been a professor of computer science at Stanford University, the former CEO of Coursera, the Chief Scientist at Baidu, the head of Google Brain, and now has his own firm, deeplearning.ai.

In the Parloff article, here's the way Andrew Ng described the impact of AI:

> "AI is the new electricity.
> Just as 100 years ago electricity
> transformed industry after industry,
> AI will now do the same."

But Professor Ng didn't mean AI in general. He meant that deep learning was the "new electricity."

Fortune took Professor Ng at his word. In the very next month, October of 2016, the magazine followed up with another article and this time reinforced the connection from AI to deep learning. The article by Geoff Colvin was entitled: *The AI Revolution: Why You Need to Learn About Deep Learning.*[2]

In April of 2018, I was in Seattle for a joint meeting of the Institute for Legal Reform of the United States Chamber of Commerce and the Chamber's recent initiative to focus on Emerging Technologies. One of the speakers said something like "Big Data is the new oil." I had heard that phrase before but this time I made the following connection, and I'm writing it for you here:

"If Big Data is the new oil, deep learning is the new refinery."

This extension makes sense, right? In a previous Revolution, oil was rare and valuable because so many products could be used with it or made from it.[3] The race was on to find it.

Now we're in the digital era of Big Data and the Data Lake has become the Data Ocean. It's turning out that while oil was hard to find, we now have the opposite problem. We're awash in Big Data and it's growing at an exponential rate. But while Big Data also can be used for valuable technological (and other) advances, it's so ever-present that we need tools to extract the insights that are business-relevant.

Of course, the business insights that matter for a company's bottom line are the ones that either drive revenue up or drive costs down. Accordingly, there are three elements for all New Refineries: hardware, software, and *business-relevant applications*. That last element is *your* opportunity.

Currently, the hardware consists of computers that combine Computing Processing Units (CPUs) with graphics processing units (GPUs), and which are optimized to run deep learning (DL) algorithms for applications (A) that matter. Thus, this Fourth Revolution consists in part of New Refineries, and they in turn consist of CPUs + GPUs + DLs + As.

But innovation for its own sake are academic research projects. While they are valuable, and move the intellectual ball forward, the applications that will be implemented must provide one or more economic benefits. In the first few chapters of *Preventing Litigation*, I presented my own research to back up my contention that reducing the frequency of litigation was a significant cost that, when avoided, would boost a company's net profits.

That may sound obvious because, for in-house counsel, the cost of litigation is often high. Worse, when asked for a budget for the coming year, the leader of corporate legal departments, the General Counsel (GC) is never at a loss for words, but is also at a loss for numbers. They know how many lawsuits were filed last year. They know how much they've spent on payouts for settlements and verdicts. They know the fees they've paid out to the law firms who represent the enterprise in litigation, deal-making, e-discovery, experts, and so on. But they have no idea how many lawsuits will be filed against the enterprise in the coming year. They also have no idea about the future mix of litigation. Perhaps they can identify a trend, as when the year-over-year onset of asbestos cases was in its early years. Beyond that, the future is opaque.

The frequency of litigation has been hard to predict because the risks have been impossible to see in advance. Now think of it: the cost of litigation is *not* a cost of goods sold or of services provided. The money spent to engage defense counsel, e-discovery vendors, and outside experts must be added to administrative costs and the money paid out in settlements and verdicts; and all of it comes straight out of net profit.

During the Tort Reform era (roughly 1995–2010), Towers Watson had accessed this data for commercial tort litigation from A. M. Best and other sources. I remember the numbers even as I write this chapter. From 2001 to 2010, the average "cost" was $160 billion per year, which means that, for 10 years, the total was $1.6 trillion. In *Preventing Litigation*, I presented my original research to show that the federal and state court caseload for that same 10-year period from 2001 to 2010 was approximately 3.909 million lawsuits. And I hasten to say "approximately" because, while the federal litigation data was front and center, the litigation data in the state courts was spotty and incomplete, even after I reached out to the National Center for State Courts. But, with extrapolations and approximations, I was able to divide $1.6 trillion by 3.9 million lawsuits and come up with ballpark cost of about $408,000 per case.

Of course, the GC who leads each company's in-house legal department may know the average cost per case for his or her enterprise. They may know, for different types of lawsuits, the trends in terms of frequency and average cost on a year-over-year basis. But to the best of my knowledge none of them share that data with the leadership of the Association of Corporate Counsel.

To me, the takeaway insight was this: *if* members of the in-house legal team could access their internal enterprise communications, they may be able to identify the "smoking guns" *in advance of getting sued* and so be able to nip the risks in the bud. They are, after all, closer to that data on a next-day basis than any attorney in any outside law firm. And if they could see and avoid just one lawsuit *per month*, then they'd help the company avoid an annual cost of about $400,000 × 12, which is nearly $5 million per year. Even when the costs of prediction/preventive deep learning software plus the cost of personnel to use the software and conduct internal investigations, are considered, the net gain was still going to be in the multiple millions of dollars.

That's business reason No. 1: save money.

Clearly, Reason No. 1 is a way to increase net profit, although not about how to increase sales and generate revenue. But decreasing cost is another way to increase net profit. If you can justify an innovation that way, why not?

Business reason No. 2 for finding a way to reduce litigation is to avoid the bad press that certain lawsuits may bring to the enterprise doorstep. That hit may be to overall reputation as in damage to the brand, or it may affect personal reputations and legacies.

That's business reason No. 2: avoid damage to brand.

Business reason No. 3 is this: Suppose an investigation by government regulators goes south and proceedings of a *criminal* nature are initiated against the company and, in some cases, one or more executives. In that case, the government must prove a specific intent to *do* harm. My thought was that a viable system for risk prevention, if implemented and operated in good faith, would be evidence of the opposite intent, a specific intent to *avoid* harm.

So business reason No. 3 is very simple: avoid jail.

But, to be sure, no risk prevention system is going to work perfectly. Companies will still get sued. But every time a lawsuit is served, the team in the legal department is obligated to send out litigation "hold" notices to anyone who might possess documents of any type that may be "potentially relevant" to the allegations in the complaint and therefore must be preserved and not destroyed.

Now put yourself in the shoes of each non-attorney who receives one of these notices. They're disturbing. The task of copying drives is hardly the end of anyone's imagination. They readily envision meeting with members of the in-house legal team and the attorneys from the law firm that represents the company. They envision getting grilled in deposition and perhaps the "joy" of testifying in front of a judge and jury. For the employees with technology educations and job functions, such musings are more like recurring nightmares and their productivity may suffer.

That's business reason No. 4. Avoid impairing employee productivity.

Of course, maybe only one of these reasons will apply when you start thinking about using deep learning for some new and innovative application. What I'm saying is that a hammer without a purpose is just a hammer.

Next, remember that a software system that uses deep learning is, in the end, just software. And, as a tool, it can be misused. And one way to misuse such software is to violate someone's privacy. Privacy is such an important issue that, even though our founders did not use the word in the U.S. Constitution, the U. S. Supreme Court found the right to privacy in the shadow or "penumbra" of the Constitution's text.

I covered this issue in Chapter 19 of *Preventing Litigation*. Here's that chapter again, updated only slightly.

I realize that employees often bring their own devices (BYOD) to work. While BYOD may be a common practice today, it is inadvisable for security purposes. Given the cost of remediating a hack into the enterprise's computer system, a company will want to protect itself from being hacked when a BYOD device is connected to the enterprise intranet. Further, because I want to identify and investigate what employees are saying to each other in order to be proactive about potential litigation threats, I see BYOD as an avoidable but significant risk.

In addition, I hasten to say, no business should invade any employee's privacy. How can a business navigate these waters?

What an Employer Should Do

Let's start with what a client should do, which is to have a "computer technology resource" (CTR) policy and to insist that each employee read and sign an Employee Manual which contains that CTR policy.

I do not mean to even suggest that I am giving legal advice, which I'm no longer entitled to give, but I think the enterprise might want to promulgate a policy something like the following:

1. Company computer and e-mail accounts should be used only for company business;

2. Employees are prohibited from sending or receiving personal e-mails, except when using a company computer to access a personal, password-protected, web-based e-mail account (for example, a personal Yahoo, Google or other e-mail account); provided, however, that if the use is so frequent and so extensive that the employee is found to be insufficiently attentive to his or her work, or disrupts the business operations of others, then the employee may be either disciplined or terminated.

3. Employees have no right to privacy with respect to any personal information or messages created on or accessed using a company computer or e-mail account;

4. E-mails sent or received on company computer resources are not private and should be regarded as postcards, and should not be understood as the equivalent of a sealed letter;

5. The company may inspect all files or messages on company computer resources at any time, for any reason, at its discretion;

6. The company or its agents may periodically monitor its computer resources and e-mail accounts to ensure compliance with its CTR policies; and

7. If any of the foregoing provisions are found to be against public policy or are unlawful, then any and all such provisions are severed from the Employee Manual, but the rest of the CTR policies and provisions shall remain in effect.

Why these elements? Because if a company follows this set of mandates, disclosures, and warnings, then, if there is no deviation from them, not even an employee's communication *with his or her personal attorney* will be entitled to privacy or privileged from discovery by the company.

Can this be? Surely the attorney-client privilege would apply to keep an employee's communication with his or her attorney privileged from disclosure, wouldn't it? The answer, if the above-listed CTR policies are in place, at least in California, is "No."

In *Holmes v. Petrovich Development Co., LLC,*[4] the appellate court noted that when the employer has an express policy which eliminates any expectation of privacy, e-mail communications between an employee and her attorney may be equivalent to "consulting her lawyer in her employer's conference room, in a loud voice, with the door open."

The facts in *Holmes* were as follows:

Gina M. Holmes ("Holmes") worked as an executive assistant for the defendants Paul Petrovich and Petrovich Development Company, LLC. After she was hired, she read and signed the company's express CTR policy that governed her usage of the company computer and e-mail account. It stated the elements I have described above.

In July 2004, approximately one month after Holmes was hired, she told Petrovich she was pregnant and wanted to take a six-week maternity leave in December. She later revised her request to a four-month maternity leave beginning in November. This prompted Petrovich to send the following e-mail to Holmes:

I need some honesty. How pregnant were you when you interviewed with me and what happened to six weeks?...That is an extreme hardship on me, my business and everyone else in the company. You have rights for sure and I am not going to do anything to violate any laws, but I feel taken advantage of and deceived for sure.

Holmes was offended and e-mailed a response that explained she did not tell him about her pregnancy earlier, in part, because she had two miscarriages in the past and did not want to disclose the pregnancy until it appeared likely that she would carry the baby to term.

Because Petrovich was concerned that Holmes may be quitting, he forwarded Holmes' e-mail to human resources and in-house counsel. When Holmes learned that Petrovich forwarded her e-mails to others, she was upset and sought legal advice concerning a claim for pregnancy discrimination.

For example, Holmes exchanged several e-mails with her attorney from her company e-mail account where she stated, "I know that there are laws that protect pregnant women from being treated differently due to their pregnancy, and now that I am officially working in a hostile environment, I feel I need to find out what rights, if any, and what options I have. I don't want to quit my job; but how do I make the situation better?"

This e-mail conflicted with Holmes's contentions at trial. At trial, her counsel objected when Petrovich's counsel tried to introduce this e-mail and other e-mails like it.

The trial court *overruled* the objections, the e-mails were admitted into evidence, and the Court of Appeals *affirmed,* holding that the employer's computer policy made clear that Holmes had no legitimate reason to believe that communications from her company e-mail account were private, regardless of whether the employer actually monitored her e-mail.

Thus, given the CTR policy, Holmes was held to have knowingly disclosed her attorney-client communications to her employer and *waived* the privilege.

Holmes is a 2011 California decision. In 2007, a New York court reached a similar conclusion. In *Scott v. Beth Israel Med. Ctr.*, the e-mail policy stated:

> "This Policy clarifies and codifies the rules for the use and protection of the Medical Center's computer and communications systems. This policy applies to everyone who works at or for the Medical Center including employees, consultants, independent contractors and all other persons who use or have access to these systems.
>
> 1. All Medical Center computer systems, telephone systems, voice mail systems, facsimile equipment, electronic mail systems, Internet access systems, related technology systems, and the wired or wireless networks that connect them are the property of the Medical Center and should be used for business purposes only.
> 2. All information and documents created, received, saved or sent on the Medical Center's computer or communications systems are the property of the Medical Center.
> Employees have no personal privacy right in any material created, received, saved or sent using Medical Center communications or computer systems. The Medical Center reserves the right to access and disclose such material at any time without prior notice."[5]

The policy was available in hard copy and maintained in the office of the administrator for each of the Center's departments and on the intranet.

The plaintiff, Dr. Scott, was the chairman of the orthopedics department and worked closely with the department administrator.

In 2002, every employee received an employee handbook which contained a brief summary of the e-mail policy. After 2002, newly hired doctors were required to sign a form acknowledging that they had read and were familiar with it.

However, Dr. Scott never signed such an acknowledgment and denied knowing of it.

Nevertheless, this "no personal use" policy, combined with a policy allowing for employer monitoring and the employee's knowledge of these two policies, diminished any expectation of privacy.

The issue materialized when Dr. Scott used Center computers to communicate by e-mail with his counsel. When Dr. Scott asserted the attorney-client privilege, the Center rejected his claim to the privilege, citing the policy.

Dr. Scott then sought a protective order from the court, but the court denied it.

In denying Dr. Scott's request for a protective order, the court cited a federal bankruptcy case, which held that the attorney-client privilege was inapplicable if:

1. "... the corporation maintain[s] a policy banning personal or other objectionable use,
2. ... the company monitor[s] the use of the employee's computer or e-mail,
3. ... third parties have a right of access to the computer or e-mails, and
4. ... the corporation notif[ies] the employee, or the employee was aware, of the use and monitoring policies."[6]

In *Scott*, the court found that the first two elements were satisfied by the Center's "no personal use" and monitoring policies; found the third element inapplicable; and held that Dr. Scott had both actual and constructive notice of the policy because the policy had been disseminated to each employee in 2002, including Dr. Scott, and because the Center made the policy available by notice on the Center's intranet.

In addition, because Dr. Scott was an administrator, he was held to have constructive notice of the policy, in part because he required newly hired doctors under his supervision to acknowledge in writing that *they* were aware of it.

As a final matter, the court rejected the argument that the attorney's notice in its e-mails to Dr. Scott changed the outcome. The notice stated:

"This message is intended only for the use of the Addressee and may contain information that is privileged and confidential. If you are not the intended recipient, you are hereby notified that any dissemination of this communication is strictly prohibited. If you have received this communication in error, please erase all copies of the message and its attachments and notify us immediately."

This (not atypical) notice appeared in every e-mail from counsel to Dr. Scott. However, the court held that the notice could not create a right of privacy out of whole cloth, and did not alter the Center's policy, stating: "When client confidences are at risk, [counsel's] pro forma notice at the end of the e-mail is insufficient and not a reasonable precaution to protect its clients."

What an Employer Should NOT Do

Given its long and venerable history, no employer should expect courts to frequently hold that the attorney-client privilege has been waived.

1. Do not undermine the policy by conduct.
   Actions often speak louder than words. Suppose that a company had a CTR policy identical to the policy described in *Petrovich*. But now suppose that the company sent the message that non-compliance would be *tolerated*. That message undermines the policy, and it is known as "operational reality."
   The "operational reality" test is used in the Ninth Circuit and was discussed in a 2008 opinion, *Quon v. Arch Wireless Operating Co.*[7]
   In *Quon*, the plaintiff had a reasonable expectation of privacy as to his personal text messages sent from his company pager because of an informal policy that contradicted the written policy. The plaintiff's supervisor had made it clear that text messages would not be audited if employees paid any applicable overage charges, even though the employer's policy prohibited the personal use of pagers.

In other words, the "operational reality" was that the plaintiff had a reasonable expectation that his personal text messages would be kept private. Thus, under those circumstances, an informal policy effectively voided the written policy.

Why can we have some confidence in the CTR policy in *Holmes?* Because Holmes argued that she had a reasonable expectation that her e-mails to her attorney were private because of the "operational reality" that the company did not audit employee computers during her employment.

But that argument failed. The Court of Appeal rejected it because there was no evidence that the company had an informal policy that contradicted its express, written policy.

The message is clear. If a company promulgates a written policy, no supervisor should undercut it with a verbal policy to the contrary.

2. Do not permit employees to use personal computer resources for work.

Holmes also argued that she had a reasonable expectation of privacy because she used a private password for her company e-mail account and deleted the e-mails after they were sent. The Court in her case also rejected this argument because Holmes had utilized her *company* e-mail account, not her *personal* e-mail account.

But suppose that the CTR policy is not clear, and an employee uses a company computer to access a personal, password-protected, web-based e-mail system to communicate with his or her attorney.

A New Jersey appellate court addressed these facts in 2010.[8] There, the plaintiff used her company issued laptop to access her Yahoo account to e-mail her attorney about bringing an employment discrimination lawsuit against her employer. The company CTR policy had *not* prohibited this.

Not surprisingly, the New Jersey court held that the attorney-client privilege had *not* been waived.

Moreover, the New Jersey court noted that a policy permitting an employer to retrieve and read an employee's attorney-client communications accessed on a *personal,* password-protected e-mail account would not be enforceable because, in New Jersey, it would be void as a matter of public policy.

3. Do not fail to have employees read and sign the policy.

Courts are reluctant to create exceptions to the attorney-client privilege, so hiccups in implementing a CTR policy can matter and
change the outcome of a case. In *Mintz v. Mark Bartelstein & Assoc.,
Inc.*, *Holmes* was distinguished by the Court, and was *not* followed
because *the employee did not read or sign the Employment Manual.*[9]
Holmes was also distinguished because the plaintiff (Mintz) used
his *home computer*, not a company device.[10] Evidently, there were
no grounds for holding the employee to constructive notice, as
in *Scott.*

Under the circumstances, the Court's ruling that Mintz had not
waived his attorney-client privilege was not unexpected. Without
requiring Mintz to read or sign the policy, and because there was no
showing that Mintz had some supervisory capacity that would have
made him aware of it, he could not be held to it.

The Internet of Things

Employers have been requiring employees to sign No Privacy policies
since 2002, if not before. But the Internet of Things (IoT)—the IoT—
did not exist in 2002. Now the future is clear: the world will be populated
with billions of smart, embedded computer devices that interact with our
personal lives, *and interact with each other.* That's the IoT.

Thus, one of the subjects of the CTR policy must be the devices that
people, in their private lives, use to access their own personal data. The
focus is not the data such devices access from the environment, that is,
the weather conditions, which is not personal to them. The focus is the
data such devices access from their own bodies, for example, such as smart
phones or watches or other kinds of wearable devices that measure tem-
perature, blood pressure, and so forth. Such data is personal, private, and
confidential to the persons who wear or otherwise carry them.

Any sensible person would see the difference between the data
collected by such personal (and so private) devices and the enterprise
computer ecosystem.

But, clearly, there is a potential for the personal device to exchange
data with an enterprise device. And so I see a two-way street: the IoT
opens a potential doorway for the enterprise to learn about an employee's

otherwise personal information, and it also opens a path for the enterprise to open itself up to a hacker attack. Given the harm due to data breaches, I can't think of a better reason for a CTR policy to ban devices known as BYODs.

So, to protect privacy as well as to protect the enterprise, employees should not be permitted to use their personal devices for work.

The Federal Trade Commission

There is yet another reason to have a CTR policy. In the context of an enterprise interacting with its customers, the Federal Trade Commission (FTC) has recently asserted a broad authority to protect the consumer. The Federal Trade Commission Act (the Act) prohibits "unfair or deceptive acts or practices in or affecting commerce," and enables the FTC as a regulatory, enforcing agency (15 U.S.C. §45(a)). The Act defines "unfair acts or practices" as acts or practices that cause or are likely to cause "substantial injury to consumers which [are] not reasonably avoidable by consumers themselves and not outweighed by countervailing benefits to consumers or to competition."[11]

For example, in a recent case, which was resolved by settlement, the FTC filed an enforcement action against TRENDNet, which makes routers, Internet cameras, and other networking devices.

The FTC alleged that TRENDNet had failed to adequately secure its Internet camera devices, which could have permitted users' live video streams to be exposed to the public. The adverse results were the litigation costs (of course), but also a requirement to revise its security policies and mandatory third-party reviews of its security obligations for the next 20 years.

In addition, there were restrictions on TRENDNet's marketing and its customer support obligations.

Now a trend is clear.[12] Businesses can expect that a failure to adopt a privacy policy (at least in the context of the data it collects from consumers), or worse, a failure to abide by its own policies, may be construed to be an *unfair and deceptive act* under the law. Accordingly, businesses should have a CTR policy in order to demonstrate that a policy existed; that it was reasonable and known to employees; and that it had been implemented and not undermined.

Notes

1. Parloff (2016).
2. Colvin (2016).
3. "Petroleum Product" (2019).
4. 191 Cal.App.4th 1047,119 Cal.Rptr.3d 878 (2011).
5. See 17 Misc. 934, 847 N.Y.S.2d 436 (2007).
6. *In re Asia Global Crossing, Ltd.*, 322 B.R.247 (S.D.N.Y. 2005).
7. *Quon v. Arch Wireless Operating Co.*, 529 F.3d 892 (9th Cir. 2008), *rev'd on other grounds by City of Ontario, Cal. v. Quon*, 560 U.S. 746, 130 S.Ct. 2619, 177 L.Ed.2d 216 (2010) (reversing on Fourth Amendment grounds only); *see also City of Ontario*, 130 S.Ct. at 2627 ("The petition for certiorari filed by Arch Wireless challenging the Ninth Circuit's ruling that Arch Wireless violated the SCA was denied.")
8. *Stengart v. Loving Care Agency, Inc.*, 990 A.2d 650 (N.J. 2010).
9. *Mintz v. Mark Bartelstein& Assoc., Inc.*, 885 F.Supp.2d 987, 998 (C.D. Cal. 2012).
10. Ibid.
11. See 15 U.S.C. 45(n). The FTC can enforce this prohibition using administrative remedies and/or judicial remedies, including in a federal court proceeding in which civil penalties and or injunctions may be sought (15 U.S.C. 45(b) and 53(b)). The FTC argued that the scope of its authority is broad because Congress intentionally did not define "unfair" and left it to the FTC to do so. See the FTC's Brief in *Federal Trade Commission v. Wyndham Hotels & Resorts, LLC*, No. 14-3514 at pp. 16–17 (3rd Cir. Nov. 14, 2014). www.ftc.gov/system/files/documents/cases/141105wyndham_3cir_ftcbrief. pdf (accessed April 8, 2015).
12. Wyndham Hotels and Resorts, LLC challenged the broadness of the FTC's authority in an interlocutory appeal to the Third Circuit. In *Federal Trade Commission v. Wyndham Hotels and Resorts, LLC*, the Third Circuit considered two issues: "whether the FTC has authority to regulate cyber security under the unfairness prong in [Section] 45(a); and, if so, whether Wyndham had fair notice its specific cyber security practices could fall short of that provision." Wyndham lost on both issues. See *Federal Trade Commission v. Wyndham Worldwide Corp.*, 799 F.3d 236 (3d. Cir. 2015). Wyndham then settled the case. The settlement required the company to establish a comprehensive information security program designed to protect cardholder data including payment card numbers, names, and expiration data. In the addition, Wyndham agreed to conduct annual information security audits and maintain safeguards in connections to its franchisees' servers. See the FTC press release dated December 9, 2015.

CHAPTER 6

Patents

I started tracking deep learning patents after December 12, 2016, the date when I was informed that my first patent would be issued. From that date, I went back in time, hoping to find a baseline. I have a spreadsheet that tracks "deep learning" patents in numerical order, beginning on January 1, 2013. It turned out that the way I was searching turned up only three or four patents during 2013, 2014, and 2015.

And by "deep learning" I mean that, in the search field of Claim(s), I track the terms "deep learning" OR "deep neural" OR "multi-layer neural."

In Figure 6.1, I present a bar chart that speaks for itself. It shows an explosion of interest in "deep learning" patents. The year-over-year results are as follows: 2013 (3), 2014 (4), 2015 (4), 2016 (36), 2017 (81), 2018 (162), through July 2, 2019 (163). Thus, at the end of the first half of 2019, the number of issued deep learning patents had already exceeded the total for 2018. It looks as if the total for 2019 may be yet another doubling of the previous year, and reach over 300 patents by the end of 2019.

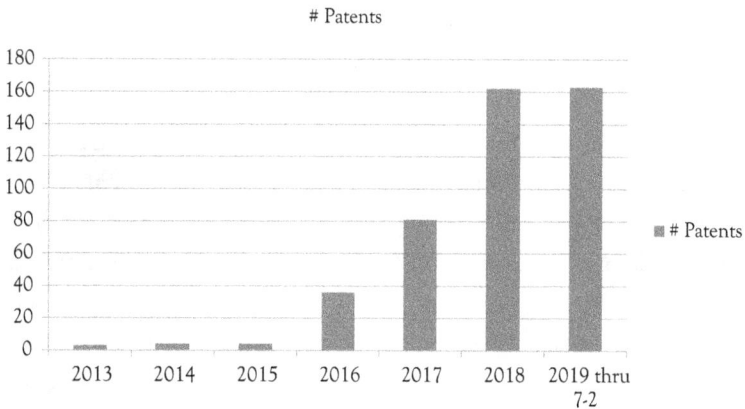

Figure 6.1 Patent "land rush" bar chart (January 1, 2013 to July 2, 2019)

As for the Leaderboard, I started tracking the names of the inventors or the corporate "assignees," that is, the owners of each patent. To keep track, I opened the link to each patent by clicking on the patent number and then, in a column separate from the patent number, recorded the name(s) of the individual inventor(s) or the name of the corporate assignee. Once I saw repetition, I created a column for that assignee. Over time, I was able to create a Leaderboard.

As of July 02, 2019, here's the Leaderboard:

1. IBM(42)
2. Google (30)
3. Microsoft (22)
3. Siemens Healthcare (22)
5. NEC (12)
6. Samsung Electronics (10)
7. Amazon (and subsidiaries) (9)
8. Adobe Systems (8)
8. INTRASPEXION (8)
10. Facebook (7)

As you can see, my patent family, assigned to Intraspexion Inc., is a sapling surrounded by a forest of Sequoias, which begs the question: Why do billion-dollar companies go after patents while startups generally don't? The answer is simple: they're established and playing a long game. Startups are focused on today and tomorrow.

Patents are expressions of an innovation, and innovations can be protected either by trade secrets, which have no expiration date if the secret is kept, or by patents. With patents, the inventor(s) or assignee(s) receive a monopoly for the innovation, as expressed by the scope of the patent's "claims," which will last for 20 years after the date the application is filed.

That said, I can't say whether Intraspexion's deep learning "patents-first" strategy is the right path for a startup. Typically, what investors want in a startup is an innovator to show that customers are buying a product because it's the solution to a problem. That's the so-called "product-market fit." My startup was swimming against that tide because, by the end of

2018, we had not found a U.S. in-house team willing to give our software system a beta test.

I had thought that corporate legal departments would want the implementing software, but I also knew that the attorneys were busy, and that they generally lacked a tech education. I also knew that they were, historically, resistant to change and probably hadn't even heard of AI or deep learning.

My bet was that corporate legal departments weren't going to be open to risk prevention until AI had become a household phrase or until the enterprise was using deep learning to such a degree that the company's in-house team would hear about it.

I believed that I was an early bird. I had been tracking deep learning patents, I could see the jump from three or four patents per year during 2013–2015 to *36* in 2016. Was this the beginning of deep learning patent land rush? I thought so. I decided to try for a patent family. A patent family may turn out to be a great Plan B.

The Petition to Make Special

I had begun my Plan B research in parallel with building a software team, and I had come to learn that I had a special patent superpower within me, so I'll tell you that story now.

As has been repeatedly reported in many publications, famed venture capitalist Vinod Khosla, at a 2011 Bangalore tech conference, warned: "People under 35 are the people who make change happen. *People over 45 basically die in terms of new ideas.*"[1]

I didn't know he'd said that. Lucky me.

On September 27, 2016, I was the sole inventor on a patent *application* for "Using Classified Text and Deep Learning Algorithms to Identify Risk and Provide Early Warning" (No. 15/277,458). I had written the specification. Obi Iloputaife, a patent attorney in Dan Cotman's IP law firm, had written the claims.

At the time, I was less than one month away from my 68th birthday.

On December 12, 2016, the USPTO issued its first Office Action (OA), which was a *Notice of Allowance* for each of the claims. Yes, you read that date correctly. The USPTO sent a Notice of Allowance only about two and a half (2½) months after the Application was filed. And, amazingly enough, on January 24, 2017, my patent issued as No. 9,552,548. That's three days shy of only *four months*. Both Dan and Obi were telling me that they had never, in over 20 years of practicing patent law, seen such speed.

Was there some "secret sauce" here? Yes. First, age didn't stop me from having new ideas. But, yes, there was something else, something about patent applications that I surfaced for myself: The Petition to Make Special.

My story of how my age accelerated my patent applications made it into the Hillsborough County Bar Association in Tampa, Florida, for the Summer of 2017.[2] The person who told it is attorney Jeff Cox. His article was entitled, "Making Your Client Special."

With that title, Jeff was referring to the Petition that Obi had filed for me along with the Application. It had a strong effect. In his article, Jeff reported that the average time for the USPTO to issue a first Office Action (OA) for the applicable class/subclass was *nine* months. His source was the USPTO itself, the USPTO's Office Action Estimator for Class = 706 and Subclass = 025000.

By receiving a first OA in less than *three* months, my application was getting special attention. Why?

The answer is that the specific document I filed with the Application was my aforementioned Petition to Make Special.[3] Now, most patent attorneys might know of a Petition to Make Special, but I doubt that *prospective inventors* are aware of it. I wasn't aware of it. I had practiced law as a litigator in California for 38 years, and assisted Dan Cotman with his patent litigation during the last two years of my career. But the subject of a Petition to Make Special never came up.

But after I thought I had come up with a "software system" invention, for risk in a general sense, I went to the USPTO home page. In the search box, I input this: "a way to expedite the review of my application."

The first result of my search was Petition Forms.

I opened the link to Petition Forms and received a result. I passed on Nos. 1, 2, and 3. Nos. 1 and 2 pertained to Abandoned Applications, while No. 3 was about a Trademark rule. But No. 4 was about a Petition to Make Special, which was a "petition to expedite initial examination of an application."

Ah ha.

I opened the link to the Petition to Make Special and found that I could not access the information without being a patent attorney.

I went back to the home page and, in the search box, and wrote "Petition to Make Special."

I opened this link and found that the second item pertained to "23—Make Special—Age and Health."

So I opened that link and found, in the third paragraph under the heading, this: "The criteria for a Petition to Make Special on the basis of Age or Health are set forth in 37 CFR **1.102**, MPEP § **708.02.**"

Now the hunt was on. Query after query was prompting me to open link after link.

To be more specific, under "Deciding Office: *The Office of Petitions*," there was this sentence: "The *criteria* for a Petition to Make Special on the basis of Age or Health are set forth in 37 CFR 1.102 MPEP § 708.02." (Italics added.)

The link to the Code of Federal Regulations (CFR) was live, so I opened it. There I found that 1.102 was for "Advancement of Examination." I'm copying out subsection(c), below. Note subsection (c)(1).

"(c) A petition to make an application special may be filed without a fee if the basis for the petition is: …. (1) *The applicant's age* or health; or…."

Of course, I wanted to know more. Seeking details, I went to the MPEP § 708.02, and found this:

II. APPLICANT'S AGE
An application may be made special upon filing a petition including any evidence showing that the applicant is *65 years of age, or more,* such as applicant's statement or a statement from a registered practitioner that he or she has evidence that the applicant is 65 years of age or older. No fee is required with such a petition. See 37 CFR 1.102(c). (Italics added.)

Eureka! That was stunning. I was already "65 years of age, or more."

I asked Obi Iloputaife about this, and, as I recall, he knew about this Petition to Make Special, and asked me for a copy of my driver's license. "That's it? Just my driver's license" I replied. Yes, he said. As with everyone's driver's license, it recited my Date of Birth.

I didn't have to do anything after that! Obi is a "registered practitioner" with the USPTO and simply stated on the form that he had seen evidence that I was 65 years of age or older.

He signed the form and no additional fee was required.

So now that you've walked in my shoes and, if you're a true inventor on a patent application *and* if you're a senior, you can avail yourself of this significant advantage of expedited processing by the USPTO. Just tell your patent counsel about a Petition to Make Special.

In my case, since I had conceived variations of the core theme of risk prevention, I followed suit with each of the six other "continuations-in-part" that I filed. We were building a patent "family." Of course, each application was accompanied by a Petition to Make Special, and each patent was approved in nine months *or less*.

In two instances, though, I was worried. I had a co-inventor on the Medical Risk patent. He was in his thirties, and definitely *not* a senior. And on the seventh continuation-in-part, which turned into the patent where blockchain is used to enable deep learning, my co-inventor was also *not* a senior.

Would that matter?

I called the Office of Petitions, connected with the reviewer who had granted my first Petition and quickly learned that the answer was no, the ages of my co-inventors would *not* derail the Petition. If I was a true co-inventor, the ages of my co-inventors *didn't matter*. My age would be sufficient grounds for the Petition to be granted.

And in these two instances, both of them were granted.

Wow. I have been looking for an edge, being curious, asking questions, and following the hints as I've shown them to you, with one clue leading to the next. It took a little work to be able to ask Obi the right question. But what a time saver!

So now, if you're a senior, you know what question to ask *your* patent counsel. And if you're much younger, you've just learned that there's a wonderful advantage to obtain when you have a senior on your innovation team. That someone, if he or she is a true inventor, can bring wisdom to the table … and speed.

Finding Patents

Now I want to switch from the application process to the substance of a patent. Before I lay out the substance of my patents, here's an alternative way to find and read them. You can readily find each of my patents because all of them have been assigned to Intraspexion. Just go to the USPTO's website, look for Find It Fast in the upper right-hand corner, click on Patents and choose "PatFT." You'll get to a search page. For Term 1, enter "Intraspexion." For Field 1, note that it's a drop-down list. Find "Assignee Name" and enter it. Or enter the abbreviation, AN. There is no need to enter anything in the boxes for Term 2 and Field 2.

Next, just below the Field 1 and Field 2 boxes, you'll find a button for Search. Click it. Intraspexion's eight patents will populate the page, in numerical order, with the highest numbered patent at the top. These are live links. Click on the Patent Number and that patent *text* (meaning the claims followed by the description) will come up, in full. Click the return arrow (top left) and you'll be back at the list and so can open the next patent.

If you're using Advanced Search, just enter AN/Intraspexion. The result will be the same.

Together, these eight patents are my current patent "family."

As I've noted, the first patent in the family is the parent to the others. The others are formally known as "continuations-in-part." Each continuation builds on the parent, so it's important for me to warn you that reading the application for the parent will take more time than any of the continuations.

As a preamble, let me say a few things about patents that I've learned from patent counsel. First, patents have several elements: An Abstract, a set of professionally written Claims; a Detailed Description of the problem and the invention as a solution (which is what you'll be writing if you're seeking a patent); and Drawings.

Typically, the description (also called a specification) lays out details. The description is specific because, when the patents expire and go into the public domain 20 years after the date of the formal patent application, some members of the public may wish to implement the invention.

The language of the claims is different. Patent *claims* are legally relevant language for discerning the scope of the patent, and they should be written by a professional to be broader than the description.

Moreover, when searching the USPTO database for Patents or Patent Applications, I recommend using the field for "Claim(s)," which is abbreviated as ACLM. When I was searching for deep learning patents, I used the following Terms: "deep learning" OR "deep neural" OR "multi-layer neural."

In the Advanced Search option, this search—where the issue date is abbreviated ISD and is shown here for 2019—would be stated as follows: ACLM/("deep learning" OR "deep neural" OR "multi-layer neural") AND ISD/2019.

I chose Claim(s) as the Field because the Claim(s) are the "metes and bounds" of a patent.[4]

Also the claim elements are typically introduced by describing "A method ... comprising" the list of elements which follows because "*comprising*" is understood to mean "including but not limited to."

And that means that if there's a claim for a part of the system that identifies a "false positive," the patent must be understood to mean a system that also identifies a "true positive" when the description and/or a diagram makes reference to both false positives and true positives.

And if the claims don't mention "retraining," but the topic is covered by the description, the claims must be understood to include retraining.

Also, when a patent is published, the text is put into a two-column format with numbers in the center and between the columns.

For example, retraining is mentioned in Col. 7 at lines 10-27 with this description:

> When a designated number of E-mails have been saved for either purpose, the positive or negative training data may be updated. In this way, the generic training data may be augmented with company-specific training data. With this additional training data, the deep learning algorithms may be re-trained in steps **120** and/ or **122** to amplify the positive or negative vector spaces for each filter, and to better reflect the enterprise's experience and culture. (Boldface in the original.)

And, in Figure 1 of the parent patent, the text of which is upcoming, the loops for training and retraining mention both false positives and true positives where step 118 leads to step 120 (false positives) and step 114 leads to step 122 (true positives).

The Parent

Now let's get to the substance of the parent patent. As a preliminary comment, the same description pertains to two patents because the text is the same in both patents, and only the claim language is different. The two patents covered by the following description are the parent, which is Patent No. 9,552,548 (issued on January 24, 2017), and my seventh, No. 9,760,850 (issued on September 12, 2017). The description is long. It lays out the statement of the problem and the solution. The "experiments" provide a "proof of concept" for the invention. I reference the drawings as Figures but include only two of them.

As a visual aid for you, I'll open each paragraph with a quotation mark and, at the very end, close the *last* paragraph with a quotation mark. I'll also signal the start of each patent's text with this phrase, "Let's begin."

Let's begin.

"This invention relates generally to machine learning and more specifically to training deep learning algorithms as text classifiers and using them to identify risks while they are still internal to the enterprise, including the risks of potential litigation.

"Overview: This invention comprises a computer-enabled software system using deep learning to identify specific, potential risks of litigation while such risks are still 'internal electronic communications' ("IECs"); that is, while the internal communications are contained on a company's computer resources, and are subject to monitoring by the company based on policies and notifications. IECs may be e-mails and any attachments thereto, a collection of call center notes, a set of warranty claims, other text documents, or transcriptions of voice mail messages. For simplicity we refer to all IECs as either e-mails (including attachments) or as "test" data. One or more embodiments of the invention relies on existing classifications of litigation data to train one or more deep learning algorithms, and then to examine IECs with them, to generate a scored output that will enable enterprise personnel, most likely attorneys or other legal department personnel, to be alerted to risks while they are still only potential lawsuits. A computer-based examination of IECs could be near real-time, e.g., overnight. After all, the purpose of an early warning system is to enable the enterprise to be proactive instead of reactive, and as soon as possible.

"Law professor Louis M. Brown (1909–1996) advocated 'preventive law.' Indeed, he pioneered this concept. His philosophy was this: 'The time to see an attorney is when you're legally healthy—certainly before the advent of litigation, and prior to the time legal trouble occurs.' He likened his approach to preventive medicine. However, Prof. Brown passed away before computer hardware and software had reached the point where his concept could be implemented. There are no conferences or journals today which focus on preventive law.

"In modern society, entities such as commercial businesses, not-for-profit organizations, governmental agencies, and other ongoing concerns (all hereinafter referred to collectively as 'enterprises') are exposed to potential liabilities if they breach contractual, criminal, governmental, or tort obligations.

"In *Preventing Litigation: An Early Warning System, Etc.* (Business Expert Press 2015) ('*Preventing Litigation*'), I presented the data showing that the average annual cost of commercial tort litigation in terms of payouts, defense attorneys' fees, and administrative expenses (collectively, 'cost'), during the 10-year period from 2001 through 2010, was $160 billion. The total cost for that 10-year timeframe was $1.6 trillion. That pain is enormous.

"In *Preventing Litigation*, I compiled the federal and state caseload for that same 10-year period, and computed the cost per case. The result was $408,000, but I concluded that the cost per case was better set at $350,000, as a minimum.

"Since litigation is neither a cost of goods sold nor a cost of services provided, this result indicates a loss to the enterprise of net gains of over $1 million for only three average commercial tort litigation matters, but it was not surprising. It is common knowledge that the cost of litigation is high. On occasion, employee misbehavior, at every level, has violated the rights of another employee, severely impaired an enterprise, harmed an entire marketplace, or physically harmed enterprise employees, members of the public, or violated their rights. However, I assert that my data compilation and calculation was the first 'per case' derivation of the average cost per case. I showed how much of a losing proposition it is for an enterprise to have to defend a commercial tort litigation matter, even if the client's attorneys are successful in the defense they mount.

"Worse, severe misconduct causing massive financial and/or physical harm may escalate to the level where criminal charges are filed. Such charges may be filed against the enterprise and the individuals responsible for the harm. In the early 1990s, the Federal Sentencing Guidelines provided benchmarks for misconduct. The Sentencing Guidelines make room for mitigating conduct and actions that speak against the heaviest penalties. In this context, a system enabling the prevention of harm may function to avoid criminal prosecution altogether. Such a system is evidence of a specific intent to *avoid* harm, which is the opposite of an element any prosecutor would be forced by law to meet: a specific intent to *do* harm.

"However, litigation can cost an enterprise in still other ways. For example, the enterprise's reputation may suffer, productivity may be reduced, as when an executive or technology employee receives a litigation hold notice and must divert his or her attention from the matters at hand; meets with in-house or outside counsel; or prepares for and then sits for a deposition or testifies in court.

"These high costs and risks are sufficient motivation to find a way to identify the risks of litigation before the damage is done. If a risk can be identified and eliminated before causing damage, the risk cannot give rise to a lawsuit. No civil lawsuit is viable without a good faith allegation of the necessary element of damages.

"The attorneys who are closest to the data internal to an enterprise are the attorneys employed by the enterprise. However, these in-house attorneys are blind to the data which contain indications of litigation risks.

"There is no software technology or product extant today which permits enterprise employees to identify and surface examples of the risks of being sued while they are still only potential legal liabilities.

"Thus, there is a need for a system capable of identifying an enterprise's own internal risks, including but not limited to the risk of litigation, and providing early warning to appropriate personnel.

"The above and other aspects, features and advantages of the invention will be more apparent from the following more particular description thereof, presented in conjunction with the following drawings wherein:

"FIG. 1 is a flow chart illustration of the process for using classified text and deep learning algorithms to identify risk and provide early warning in accordance with one or more embodiments of the present invention.

"FIG. 2 illustrates a general-purpose computer and peripherals that when programmed as described herein may operate as a specially programmed computer capable of implementing one or more methods, apparatus and/or systems of the present invention.

"FIG. 3 is a bar graph illustration of e-mail score frequencies above 0.80 for 400 training documents.

"FIG. 4 is a bar graph illustration of e-mail score frequencies after training to find employment discrimination risks.

"FIG. 5 is a graph of Receiver Operating Characteristic (ROC) and related Area Under the Curve (AUC)."

"The present invention comprising using classified text and deep learning algorithms to identify risk and provide early warning will now be described. In the following exemplary description numerous specific details are set forth in order to provide a more thorough understanding of embodiments of the invention. It will be apparent, however, to an artisan of ordinary skill that the present invention may be practiced without incorporating all aspects of the specific details described herein. Furthermore, although steps or processes are set forth in an exemplary order to provide an understanding of one or more systems and methods, the exemplary order is not meant to be limiting. One of ordinary skill in the art would recognize that one or more steps or processes may be performed simultaneously or in multiple process flows without departing from the spirit or the scope of the invention. In other instances, specific features, quantities, or measurements well known to those of ordinary skill in the art have not been described in detail so as not to obscure the invention. It should be noted that although examples of the invention are set forth herein, the claims, and the full scope of any equivalents, are what define the metes and bounds of the invention.

"For a better understanding of the disclosed embodiment, its operating advantages, and the specified object attained by its uses, reference should be made to the accompanying drawings and descriptive matter in which there are illustrated exemplary disclosed embodiments. The disclosed embodiments are not intended to be limited to the specific forms set forth herein. It is understood that various omissions and substitutions of equivalents are contemplated as circumstances may suggest or render expedient, but these are intended to cover the application or implementation.

"The term 'first', 'second' and the like, herein do not denote any order, quantity or importance, but rather are used to distinguish one element from another, and the terms 'a' and 'an' herein do not denote a limitation of quantity, but rather denote the presence of at least one of the referenced item. The terms 'e-mail' and 'E-mail' both refer to an e-mail and any attachment.

"The term 'algorithm' refers to a 'deep learning algorithm,' 'deep learning neural network,' or a 'deep learning model,' all of which here refer to a form of text classification.

"One or more embodiments of the present invention will now be described with references to FIGS. 1–5. (Figure 6.1 is the same as FIG. 1 in the patent.)

"FIG. 1 is a flow chart illustration of the process 100 for using classified text and deep learning algorithms to identify risk and provide early warning. As illustrated, the process 100 begins at block 102 with mining of data for training one or more deep learning algorithms. In the typical instance, subject matter experts identify one or more datasets with classifications of risk or threats having a sufficient number of textual documents. These classifications (or categories or labels) of risk are more typically from sources outside of the enterprise. The system datamines such classified datasets to extract a sufficient number of documents within a specific category to train one or more deep learning algorithms.

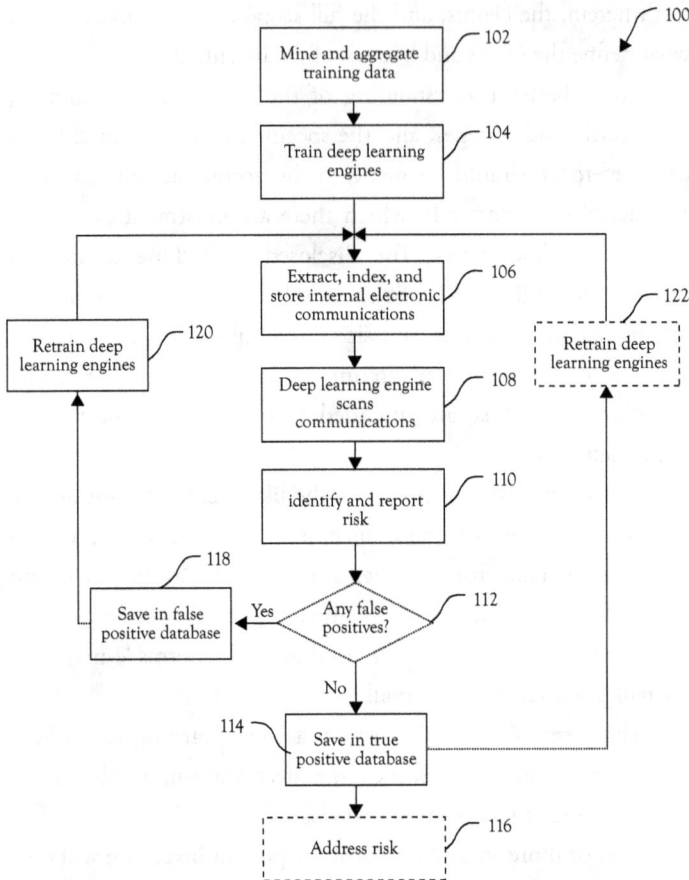

Figure 6.2 This is FIG. 1 in Patent No. 9,552,548

"In the context of litigation risk, for example, a subject matter expert would note that the federal court litigation database known as the Public Access to Court Electronic Records (PACER) is based on well over one hundred case types, to which PACER assigns Nature of Suit (NOS) codes. When a federal court lawsuit is initiated, the person filing it must complete and file a form called a Civil Cover Sheet, which instructs the person responsible for filing the lawsuit to review a list of NOS codes and choose one and only one code which best describes the lawsuit, even if there is more than one theory of recovery.

"To create a set of training documents for a particular federal court litigation risk, a user of this invention would use PACER's Application Programming Interface (API) to obtain hundreds if not thousands of text documents from previous lawsuits which have been filed in a specific NOS category. Such a user would then compile a large number of training documents which describe the facts (not the law) which prompted the lawsuit to be filed in the first place.

"In this illustrative example, PACER would be a generic source of classified text outside of the enterprise, which is as training data. A ready (but not the only) source of training data is a lawsuit complaint in a specific case-type category, as identified by its NOS category name or number.

"NOS categories are not difficult to understand. One of them, for example, is the category of Civil Rights-Employment which, in other words, means illegal discrimination against employees, whether it is for age, race, sex, or some other subclass of illegal discrimination. In addition, and among over one hundred categories, there are codes for breach of contract, fraud and product liability case-types.

"There may be other sources of training data, i.e., internal enterprise sources of specific litigation case-type training data. Some examples are: textual data from the previous litigation history of an enterprise; text in warranty claims; and data from the confirmation by a user that a specific system output document (e.g., e-mail) has been scored by the algorithm in a way indicating that it should be saved and used for re-training the algorithm.

"Using litigation case-type data, a complaint is usually (but not always) identified as the first document in a litigation docket, i.e., Document Number 1. In order to train a deep learning algorithm, the focus is on the factual allegations in these complaints. These factual allegations may be stated in a section of a complaint entitled 'Background Facts' or the like.

"Many sections of a complaint are unnecessary and consist of legalistic statements that can be deleted for the purpose of training the algorithm. For example, the sections that pertain to jurisdiction, venue, the identification of the parties, the legal theories for recovery, and the prayer for damages are unnecessary. By deleting unnecessary text, the amount of training data is reduced, and the training data will contain less "noise" for analysis by the deep learning algorithm.

"In some cases, the plaintiff in a case may be represented by an attorney. In that case, the fact section is based on information provided by the attorney's client and by the information stemming from the attorney's research. Because attorneys typically present facts in a logical way, so as to be both understood and persuasive, we assume that such facts have been vetted. For this reason, complaints written by counsel are a prime source of training data.

"However, additional facts may be developed after the complaint is filed and during the discovery of electronically stored information, e.g., by way of production of documents, responses to written interrogatories, or by testimony given during depositions and the like. Although such facts are generally not placed in the public record, certain key facts are put into the public record (e.g., in PACER) as part of motions for summary judgment.

"The data mining needed to create a strong deep learning algorithm aims at surfacing a large number of factual allegations within a specific risk case-type.

"In one or more embodiments, the system's primary, but not only, source of training data consists of the facts alleged in previously filed complaints filed in a specific category of lawsuit.

"Such litigation data is *positive* training data, and typically contains no e-mails. The risks the system of the present invention would seek to surface test data that would be 'related' to the aggregation of these positive facts. The degree of the relation is reported by an accuracy score ranging from 0.50 to a maximum of 1.0. The training data also includes *negative* training data, such as text concerning some unrelated topic, e.g., the Holy Roman Empire. (Negative, unrelated training data may be obtained from Wikipedia, for example.) The system uses negative training data to better score test data as either related or unrelated to a specific case-type.

"The training data is crucial for a deep learning engine to be able to produce an accuracy score for the text in the *test* data, which typically consists primarily of e-mails. The algorithm can produce an accuracy score by comparing an e-mail, as encoded, to the vector space described by the positive training data related to the risk, and to the negative training data, which is unrelated.

"The process of aggregating this training material and providing it to a deep learning engine involves creating a 'vector' for each word in the block in relation to the two or three words before and after it. Accordingly, each word vector has its own context, and that context is meaningful in connection with the type of case (and the type of risk) for which the deep learning algorithm is being trained. Transforming the text used in a specific classification (or, for litigation, specific category or type of case) into numerical vectors may be accomplished via various methods such as Word2vec by Tomas Mikolov at Google, 'GloVe: Global Vectors for Word Representation' by Jeffrey Pennington, et al., etc.

"However, to make the matter clear, although the deep learning algorithm will encode the text in the above-described manner, i.e., words within the context of other words, the factual allegations are not provided to the algorithm word by word, sentence by sentence, or paragraph by paragraph. Instead, the whole block of factual allegations is presented for ingestion as a document.

"One object of amassing a sufficient number (hundreds if not thousands) of training documents is to train a deep learning algorithm so that it functions well, and so is considered 'strong.' Consequently, at step 104, category-specific training documents are passed to, and ingested by, one or more deep learning algorithms best suited to handle natural language processing (NLP). The algorithm more commonly used in the context of NLP and text analysis is known to practitioners in the art as a recurrent neural networks (RNN).

"Such deep learning RNNs use hidden computational 'nodes' and various 'gates,' and require manipulation known in the art as 'tuning.' After the process of 'tuning,' the algorithm will be evaluated to assess the degree to which it accurately identifies the textual test data it has never before encountered with the 'vector space' it has been trained to recognize. As one example, practitioners construct a ROC graph and calculate the AUC score. An ROC graph measures true positives (on the y-axis) versus false positives (on the x-axis). Because the maximum AUC score is one (1.0), an ROC-AUC score in the mid-nineties, e.g., 0.95, indicates that there are far more true positives than false positives. In experiments, described below, the RNNs of the present invention have achieved scores above 0.967.

"When an algorithm is trained to 'understand' a particular type of case, it may be thought of as a 'filter.' Typically, the system will consist of more than one filter. The system passes the enterprise data through each filter. The reason is clear: A deep learning algorithm trained to identify 'breach of contract' risks, which we now call a filter, may find no risk in the test data, but an 'employment discrimination' filter may find one or more high-scoring e-mails in the same data.

"Once the Deep Learning Engine is trained, at step 106 the system indexes and also extracts text from each E-mail and in any attachment. Those of skill in the art will appreciate that other implementations are contemplated. For example, it may be necessary or desirable to only extract the subject line and the unstructured text in the message field. In addition, the indexed data may be stored for a specific period of time in a database, a period which the Enterprise may designate in accordance with its data destruction policies.

"In one or more embodiments, the system at step 106 may operate in a non-real-time mode by extracting existing internal e-mail data, e.g., from the previous day's E-mail, and then stores the data in a database. In other embodiments, the system at step 106 may operate in real-time to intercept, index, store, and extract text from internal E-mail data.

"After indexing, extracting text, and storing the internal E-mail data in a database, the system passes that data to each of the category-specific algorithms at step 108, which are also referred to herein as 'filters.' Each filter scores the data for each E-mail for accuracy in comparison to how each filter was trained.

"Once each E-mail is scored for accuracy in relation to the risks or threats by one of the filters, the score and text are output at step 110. The E-mails related to a particular risk may be reported as an 'early warning' alert to specific employees, for example. These employees may be a pre-determined list of in-house attorneys, paralegals or other employees in the legal department.

"In addition, an enterprise may configure the system to send its 'early warning' alert to a list of devices owned by the enterprise where the communication of the output may be encrypted using appropriate security measures.

"When a scored E-mail is reported to a designated enterprise employee, that employee may be enabled to review the E-mail in one or more of several modes, e.g., the scored text in a spreadsheet format and/or a bar graph distribution. Using the spreadsheet format, after reviewing a row of score and E-mail text, a user may call that E-mail to the fore and review it in its native state. This feature is possible because the E-mails were indexed when they were copied into the system.

"At step 112, when a determination is made, e.g., by a reviewer such as an attorney or paralegal, that a specific E-mail is, at least provisionally, a false positive (and that further investigation is not warranted), the process proceeds to step 118 where the e-mail is stored in a False Positive database. A user interface, e.g., graphical, may be provided for the reviewer to perform the necessary designations, for example. Those of skill in the art would appreciate that the system could be configured to perform this determination step automatically, with the reviewer having a veto or override capability, for example.

"However, if at step 112 a determination is made that an identified E-mail is a true positive, a copy of that E-mail may be placed in a True Positive database at step 114. When a designated number of E-mails have been saved for either purpose, the positive or negative training data may be updated. In this way, the generic training data may be augmented with company-specific training data. With this additional training data, the deep learning algorithms may be re-trained in steps 120 and/or 122 to amplify the positive or negative vector spaces for each filter, and to better reflect the enterprise's experience and culture.

"E-mail marked as true positive and placed in True Positive database at step 114 may be exported via an API to the enterprise's existing litigation or investigation case management system at step 116, if any, from which the risk may be optionally addressed. The algorithm's positive output may be limited to scores which surpass a user-specified threshold, for example.

"The system of the invention we have now described has two additional advantages. The first advantage is confidentiality. If the enterprise directs its legal department to install the system and have its attorneys direct and control its operation, including any involvement by the IT department, then the attorneys using the system may invoke the attorney work-product doctrine. Then, when the system provides an output to a designated list of attorneys or other legal department personnel, such as paralegals, the enterprise may again invoke the attorney-work product doctrine when someone in the legal department decides which e-mails to investigate. Similarly, the work-product doctrine should apply when legal department personnel use an API to access and use whatever case or investigation management platform the enterprise uses.

"In addition, when an investigation appears to warrant further action of a proactive, preventive nature, the enterprise attorneys may advise a control group executive in order to invoke the attorney-client privilege.

"Thus, by installing and operating the system in the manner described above, the invention provides confidentiality to the sensitive information that is being brought to light.

"The second advantage arises whenever a regulatory investigation becomes problematic. Should a governmental entity file criminal charges against the enterprise and or any of its personnel, the prosecuting authorities will have to present evidence of a specific intent to do harm. But by installing and operating the system of this invention in good faith, the enterprise and anyone so charged will have countervailing evidence of a specific intent to avoid harm.

To summarize: Once the deep learning algorithm is trained, the system has three major subsystems, enterprise data, the deep learning algorithms or filter(s), and the output data. Taken together, the system operates to identify a potentially adverse risk to the enterprise and provide early warning to a user. In the exemplary embodiments provided herein, the potentially adverse risk is the risk of a specific type of litigation but could just as well be other types of risk, including the risk of physical harm to the enterprise's customers by the enterprise's products.

"**FIG. 2** diagrams a general-purpose computer and peripherals 200, when programmed as described herein, may operate as a specially programmed computer capable of implementing one or more methods, apparatus and/or systems of the solution described in this disclosure. Processor 207 may be coupled to bi-directional communication infrastructure 202 such as communication infrastructure system bus 202. Communication infrastructure 202 may generally be a system bus that provides an interface to the other components in the general-purpose computer system such as processor 207, main memory 206, display interface 208, secondary memory 212 and/or communication interface 224.

"Main memory 206 may provide a computer readable medium for accessing and executed stored data and applications. Display interface 208 may communicate with display unit 210 that may be utilized to display outputs to the user of the specially-programmed computer system. Display unit 210 may comprise one or more monitors that may visually depict aspects of the computer program to the user. Main memory 206 and display interface 208 may be coupled to communication infrastructure 202, which may serve as the interface point to secondary memory 212 and communication interface 224. Secondary memory 212 may provide additional memory resources beyond main memory 206, and may generally function as a storage location for computer programs to be executed by processor 207. Either fixed or removable computer-readable media may serve as Secondary memory 212. Secondary memory 212 may comprise, for example, hard disk 214 and removable storage drive 216 that may have an associated removable storage unit 218. There may be multiple sources of secondary memory 212 and systems implementing the solutions described in this disclosure may be configured as needed to support the data storage requirements of the user and the methods described herein. Secondary memory 212 may also comprise interface 220 that serves as an interface point to additional storage such as removable storage unit 222. Numerous types of data storage devices may serve as repositories for data utilized by the specially programmed computer system. For example, magnetic, optical, or magnetic-optical storage systems, or any other available mass storage technology that provides a repository for digital information may be used.

"Communication interface 224 may be coupled to communication infrastructure 202 and may serve as a conduit for data destined for or received from communication path 226. A network interface card (NIC) is an example of the type of device that once coupled to communication infrastructure 202 may provide a mechanism for transporting data to communication path 226. Computer networks such Local Area Networks (LAN), Wide Area Networks (WAN), Wireless networks, optical networks, distributed networks, the Internet or any combination thereof are some examples of the type of communication paths that may be utilized by the specially program[ed] computer system. Communication path 226 may comprise any type of telecommunication network or interconnection fabric that can transport data to and from communication interface 224.

"To facilitate user interaction with the specially programmed computer system, one or more human interface devices (HID) 230 may be provided. Some examples of HIDs that enable users to input commands or data to the specially programmed computer may comprise a keyboard, mouse, touch screen devices, microphones or other audio interface devices, motion sensors or the like, as well as any other device able to accept any kind of human input and in turn communicate that input to processor 207 to trigger one or more responses from the specially programmed computer are within the scope of the system disclosed herein.

"While **FIG. 2** depicts a physical device, the scope of the system may also encompass a virtual device, virtual machine or simulator embodied in one or more computer programs executing on a computer or computer system and acting or providing a computer system environment compatible with the methods and processes of this disclosure. In one or more embodiments, the system may also encompass a cloud computing system or any other system where shared resources, such as hardware, applications, data, or any other resource are made available on demand over the Internet or any other network. In one or more embodiments, the system may also encompass parallel systems, multi-processor systems, multi-core processors, and/or any combination thereof. Where a virtual machine, process, device or otherwise performs substantially similarly to that of a physical computer system, such a virtual platform will also fall within the scope of disclosure provided herein, notwithstanding the description herein of a physical system such as that in **FIG. 2**.

"Embodiments of the present invention were validated using training data for the employment discrimination case-type, two similar (but different) deep learning algorithm providers, and a portion of Ken Lay's Enron e-mail corpus. The system found one (1) risky e-mail out of 7,665 e-mails.

"The system as described herein requires multiple types of factual information. For example, the factual information may include but is not limited to a compilation of factual allegations previously presented as pre-litigation demands; a compilation of factual allegations previously presented as part of filed lawsuits; factual details extracted from hypothetical examples of potential legal liability as identified and preserved by authorized personnel; factual details extracted from learned treatises; factual details from employee complaints; and factual details from customer complaints.

"First, text data from prior court cases (and other sources) pertaining to employment discrimination lawsuits were extracted as an example of many case-types. Second, the text data was used to train two deep learning algorithms in two ways, with documents that were related to prior employment discrimination lawsuits, and with documents that were clearly *not* related to an employment discrimination risk. There were no e-mails in the training data.

"Next, as trained, the deep learning algorithms were presented with test data consisting of a portion of the Enron e-mail subset for Ken Lay, the former Chairman and CEO of Enron. The test data consisted of only these e-mails.

"Before the experiments, the PACER database was reviewed for statistics about Enron. For the five-year period 1997–2001, the chances of finding a workplace discrimination case against an Enron company was only about one percent (1%). During that five-year timeframe, an Enron company was named in litigation 1,339 times, and was named in an employment discrimination case only 13 times. Accordingly, there was no expectation of a significant result because it is unlikely that employees with a discrimination complaint would reach out to Ken Lay. Ken Lay was, after all, the Chairman and CEO of Enron, not a manager and not the director of Human Resources.

"Next, PACER was data-mined to extract certain text portions of documents filed in the employment discrimination category to create a set of training documents in this silo.

"The first experiment was with a deep learning algorithm provided by MetaMind, which was later acquired by Sales force. The amount of training data was increased in baby steps. The first experiment used only 50 training documents, but provided immediate results, which was surprising and unexpected, in part because Ken Lay was the Chairman and CEO of Enron, not the director of the Human Resources department.

"As configured for the experiment, the system reported the results in two formats. The first format is an Excel spreadsheet. There, in the first row, in Column A, the system shows the scores which indicate the accuracy of the E-mail text compared to the case-type for which the algorithm was trained. In Column B, the system shows a portion of the E-mail text associated with the score. Twenty-two (22) e-mails were found which scored at 0.90 or above for accuracy out of 6,352 e-mails, and two of them expressed a risk of employment discrimination, with one being a 'forward' of the other.

"The second format is a bar graph of the data scored by the algorithm, illustrated in Figure 3. The bar graph is a distribution which provides context for the highest scoring e-mails. On the x-axis, the bar graph shows the scores for the e-mails. The highest possible score is 1.0 and is on the far right. On the y-axis, the graph shows the number of e-mails which received any particular score. The distribution bar graph only shows the scores ranging from 0.80 to 1.00.

"In reviewing the top-scoring 22 e-mails, i.e., the ones which scored 0.90 or above, the data showed that most of them were false positives, but two e-mails (as noted above) stood out. Scoring at 0.94, both of them presented a discrimination risk, but it was the same risk, because one e-mail was a 'forward' of the initial version. The subject of that e-mail was '[M]y unfair treatment at Enron--Please HELP.'

"After further training, to 400 documents, the number of false positives was reduced. The deep learning algorithm scored only four (4) e-mails at 0.86 or higher.

"In the resulting spreadsheet, lines 3 and 4 scored at the 0.86 and 0.88 levels respectively. Those e-mails include the phrase 'my unfair treatment at Enron.' Upon further review, the first paragraph of the e-mail in the spreadsheet began: 'Dear Mr. Lay, [M]y employment with Enron *is to be terminated, the reason given by HR, for not meeting performance standards.* However, I firmly believe that this is not the real reason, the real one being for defying the wishes of my manager ..., *who, I believe was acting in a discriminatory way towards me....*' (italics added.)

"As the number of our training documents increased, it became evident that the deep learning algorithm was becoming more accurate. In addition, the inclusion of a negative dataset (and vector space), e.g., pertaining to the Holy Roman Empire and calendar entries, also reduced the number of false positives in the results.

"Further experiments with a list of sex and race terms demonstrated that they added little to the strength of the algorithm if anything. This may be because the lists lacked any context and were as insufficient as any list of key words.

"In the experiment pertaining to the spreadsheet where four high-scoring E-mails were identified, about 400 training documents were used. As previously mentioned, only *four* e-mails scored at or above 0.80 for accuracy with respect to the training data. Two e-mails scored above 0.90 for accuracy, while the other two scored 0.88 and 0.86. In a subsequent experiment using 7,665 Ken Lay e-mails, the distribution bar graph for this experiment is illustrated in Figure 4. The y-axis runs from 0 to only 12, indicating that the deep learning algorithm was now much more focused.

"The experiments also showed that a deep learning algorithm, however well trained, will nevertheless generate an alert that a reviewer would reject for follow up. For example, the E-mail scoring at 0.97 was from an Enron employee in India. In part, it read: 'Subsequently, I was forced upon a cheque of severance amount on 27th August 2001 which I received under protest and the notice of such protest was served by me on firm in the interest of justice. I submit such a termination is illegal, bad in law and void ab-initio and accordingly *when such an action was not corrected by firm, I [was] constrained to approach the Court of law.*' (italics added.)

"Thus, while that E-mail recounts a discrimination risk, the risk appears to have already become a lawsuit. A reviewing attorney might well consider this high-scoring e-mail to be a false positive, especially if he or she determines that a lawsuit has already been filed.

"A second experiment used Indico Data Systems, Inc. ('Indico') Deep Learning Algorithm to validate the previous training with MetaMind. Indico was provided with the same training data used with MetaMind and with the same test data.

"The results showed that the same risky E-mail found using MetaMind that had text in the subject line stating, 'unfair treatment at Enron,' which 0.86 and 0.88 with MetaMind, was

ROC plot for cross-validated models

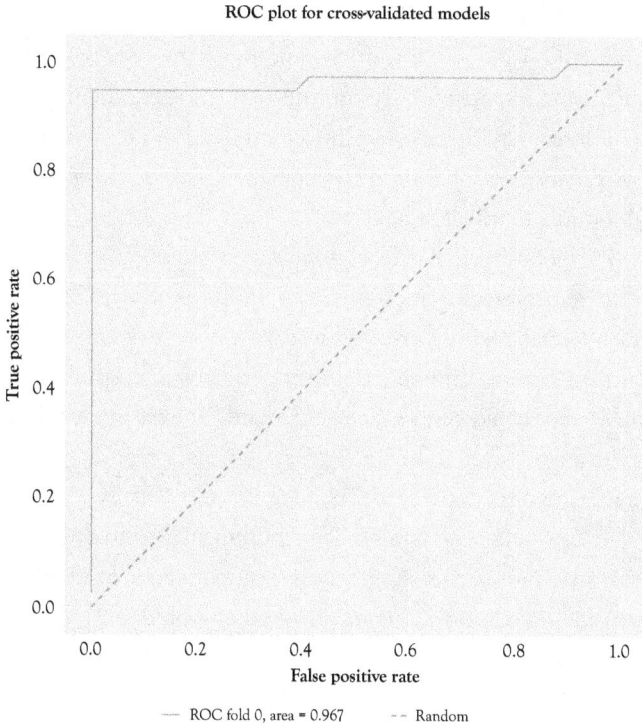

— ROC fold 0, area = 0.967   - - Random

*Figure 6.3 This ROC-AUC graph above is FIG. 5 in Patent
No. 9,552,548*

flagged Indico's model, and the same E-mail scored 0.89, which
is comparable.

"Indico also used about 75 held-out documents in order to
provide a graph of a curve showing a ROC, illustrated in FIG. 5,
which included a related indicator called the AUC. These statistics
put 'true positives' on the y-axis and 'false positives' on the x-axis.
On both axes, the maximum score is 1.0. A strong algorithm will
score high and to the left, which is what we saw.

"Also since the maximum score for each axis is 1.0, the area
under the ROC curve is also 1.0. According to the second provider, Indico, the AUC score was 0.967 (see the AUC score in
the lower right hand corner), which means that the algorithm, as
trained, is strong.

"In these experiments, the early warning system, having been
trained (as an example) to detect an employment discrimination

risk, found one (1) e-mail out of 7,665 e-mails which signaled just such a risk. Thus, the inventive concept of the system has been tested using a specific litigation category, the same training data, two different algorithms, and Enron test data, and has functioned in accordance with the inventive concept. The system, as trained, had found a needle in a haystack.

"Furthermore, the early warning system would function for an authorized enterprise employee in an unobtrusive way. Enterprise personnel need not be involved in data-mining to train the Deep Learning system, and the algorithm itself would scan internal e-mails and would run in the background. The system would not require anyone's attention until the system had a reportable result, at a threshold the legal department could set.

"At that point, the system would output an alert to a privileged list of in-house personnel, likely in-house counsel or employees under their direction and control, and they would be able to see a spreadsheet with a score in column A, the related text in column B, along with a bar chart for context, and then would be enabled to call forward the E-mails of interest.

"The experiments discussed above employed deep learning algorithms which are described in the academic literature as Recursive Neural Tensor Networks or as RNNs with either Long Short-Term Memory (LSTM) or Gated Recurrent Units (GRUs). Those of skill in the arts will appreciate that use of other algorithms, including those which are now open-sourced, are contemplated.

"While the invention herein disclosed has been described by means of specific embodiments and applications thereof, numerous modifications and variations could be made thereto by those skilled in the art without departing from the scope of the invention set forth in the claims."

An Example of Claims

Note that the last paragraph indicated that the "scope of the invention" was "set forth in the claims." I think I'd be remiss if I didn't recite some of the claim language for the "parent" as an example. Before I do that, there were 20 claims. Some of them are stand-alone, like Claim **1**, but many of them refer to a previous claim. And, while the description of the invention is stated in the context of a litigation risk, Claim **1** is much broader, and defines the scope of the invention as "[a] risk classification [that] comprises one or more threats or risks of interest." To give you the idea, I'll recite Claims **1** and **2** of the parent patent:

"What is claimed is:

1. A method of using classified text and deep learning algorithms to identify risk and provide early warning comprising:
   • creating one or more training datasets for textual data corresponding to one or more risk classifications, wherein said risk classification comprises one or more threats or risks of interest;
   • training one or more deep learning algorithms using said one or more training datasets;
   • extracting an internal electronic communication of an enterprise;
   • applying said one or more deep learning algorithms to said internal electronic communication to identify and report any one of said one or more threats or risks of interest;
   • determining if said identified one of said one or more threats or risks of interest is a false positive or a true positive;
   • re-training said one or more deep learning algorithms if said identified one of said one or more threats or risks of interest is a false positive; and
   • saving said internal electronic communication in a true positive database if said identified one or said one or more threats or risks of interest is a true positive.

2. The method of Claim **1**, wherein said one or more deep learning algorithms is a framework for natural language processing of text."

Notes

1. Wadhwa (2011).
2. Cox (2017).
3. 37 CFR 1.102(c)(1). See also M.P.E.P § 708.02, Section IV.
4. USPTO (United States Patent and Trademark Office) (2019).

CHAPTER 7

Continuations

My second patent, No. 9,754,205, was issued on September 5, 2017. For this and the other "continuations," the text of the parent is the foundation. For a continuation, there's new text that starts *after* the text for the parent ends. Thus, the text for a continuation is the only new material. To provide you with these examples, I'm presenting only the additional text of the variation on the theme. As before, a set of closing double quotes indicates the end of the continuation text.

Dangerous Documents

Let's begin.

"Here, deep learning is used to identify specific, potential risks to an enterprise (of which product liability is the prime example here) while such risks are still internal electronic communications (IECs). The system involves mining and using existing classifications of data (e.g., from an internal litigation database, or from external sources such as customer complaints, and/or warranty claims) to train one or more deep learning algorithms, and then examining the enterprise's IECs with the trained algorithm, to generate a scored output that will enable enterprise personnel to be alerted to risks and take action in time to prevent the risks from resulting in harm to the enterprise or others.

"The difficulty of addressing this category of litigation is high. Product liability lawsuits are based on a strict liability theory. Generally, a plaintiff only knows that he or she has been injured and by what product. All of these facts are post-sale of the product and external to the enterprise. Hence, in the absence of a whistleblower, product liability lawsuits generally have no factual allegations as to facts internal to the enterprise.

"The system remains text based. The external training data consists of the text in warranty claims and/or the text associated with customer complaints to the enterprise or from call centers. Such information should be directed to the legal department before moving inward. To the best of the inventor's knowledge, this work flow does not exist currently and the risks go undetected. However, such claims and/or complaints may include signals of product deficiencies. Such signals would put legal department employees on the hunt for the internal training data which, in part, consists of 'dangerous documents.'

"A 'dangerous document' is the appellation given to one or more internal communication wherein competing goals are at odds in ways that are potentially dangerous to the enterprise, e.g., when the desire for safety is compromised by a desire for profit or a desire to save time (or avoid a delay). The combination exposes the enterprise to product liability litigation, which is why the system of the present invention is warranted.

"The following example explains the concept of a 'dangerous document.' Suppose that an enterprise engineer reports to her manager that a supplier has unexpectedly switched to a cheaper but flammable material, such that the product no longer meets the specifications for being not flammable, as intended and advertised. She recommends further testing, manufacturing changes, and a recall of the tens of thousands of defective units already shipped with the out-of-specification material. Her manager responds by telling the engineer that she (the manager) is here to bank profits for the company, not incur unexpected costs; and that the engineer is never to use the term 'defect' and instead should use only the phrase 'does not meet specifications.' The manager ends by telling the engineer to meet her for lunch instead of replying by e-mail. (This example is partially drawn from a *Wall Street Journal* blog article in May of 2014 by Tom Gara entitled 'The 69 Words You Can't Use at GM.')

"Returning to the external documents, the problem with warranty claims is that they are too often evaluated as to whether the claim should be accepted or rejected, with no further action taken. In the same vein, enterprises often only want to know whether customers who make complaints, e.g., to call centers, are either satisfied or not satisfied, in varying degrees, by the enterprise response.

"However, the external information provided by customers in warranty claims or customer complaints is valuable to the enterprise both as training data for product liability risk and as test data.

"In this variation, the enterprise corporate legal department deploys and operates the system. In the end, the role of corporate counsel will expand to include deciding whether to initiate an internal product liability risk investigation, and then, where warranted, to advise technical control group executives, i.e., executives with engineering, science, or technology oversight and decision-making responsibilities, that *external* communications by customers are indicating a risk which may prompt them to conduct an internal investigation into whether risky *internal* communications exist.

"Risky internal communications comprises IECs between technical personnel, on the one hand, or between one or more technical employees and one or more managers, on the other.

"As training data for a deep learning algorithm, warranty claims, customer complaints, in the form of either paper or audio inputs, and 'dangerous documents' extracted from previous and now-closed product liability lawsuits, may be digitized, translated, transformed into text, aggregated, and converted to number strings by using a word-embedding technique such as word2vec or GloVe, as previously indicated. However, in the case previous product liability lawsuits have been settled using agreements with confidentiality provisions, the training text need not be specific, and, where confidentiality provisions exist, must not contain customer, employee, and product names and must be redacted unless viewed only by enterprise personnel. Even where confidentiality provisions are not evident, and third parties may view the training data, names of customers, employees, and products constitute 'noise' in the data and are best redacted.

"Such text-based data is suitable for input to an RNN-type deep learning algorithm as training data.

"Once an algorithm has been trained by using external and/or internal sources, it can then score *internal* risky e-mails, just as the system of the present invention instructs, and output to users the algorithm scores and IECs in displays which alert and augment the intelligence of the users as to whether a product liability risk exists or not.

"In this way, the enterprise users, be they legal or technical personnel, may receive an early warning of a defect or similar issue with a particular product. In the event a recall is necessary, the number of units will, potentially, be far less than the number of units that would have to be recalled if the deficiencies noted by customers remain undetected.

"Thus, with an early warning from either external sources or from the legal department, technical personnel will be able to address the design and manufacturing issues raised by the claims and/or complaints sooner rather than later.

"While the invention herein disclosed has been described by means of specific embodiments and applications thereof, numerous modifications and variations could be made thereto by those skilled in the art without departing from the scope of the invention set forth in the claims."

Contract Failure

My third patent is No. 9,754,206. It was issued right after the previous patent which is why the number is sequential. The issue date is the same: September 5, 2017.

Let's begin.

"In this variation, one example of a drafting flaw in a document is ambiguity. In a contract, ambiguity may be fatal if incurable by reference to conduct or in some other way, because the parties may have failed to have a 'meeting of the minds.'

"Using the system of the invention, and with the ambiguity flaw as the focus, a Deep Learning algorithm would be trained with examples of appellate decisions in the PACER database, and other, similar sources, in which a contract is the subject of a dispute and the issue is whether the source of the dispute is whether the language of a provision is ambiguous.

"Using various sources of such appellate rulings, and as a matter of data-mining the factual recitations by a court in such cases, such ambiguous contract provisions themselves may be identified, along with some amount of text before and after the court discussions pertaining to that drafting flaw.

"Once such appellate decisions are identified, the court opinions (and concurring opinions if they deal with the same subject) may be aggregated into a set of training documents.

"The Deep Learning algorithms of the present invention may be trained with such documents to identify documents related to that risk, along with other documents unrelated to it. Documents unrelated to documents which may fail to create contractual obligations may consist of documents with text for a wholly different purpose such as, e.g., news reports, poetry, or science fiction short stories.

"Thereafter, the algorithms trained for various specific drafting flaws may be made accessible to attorneys and paralegals who focus their practice on drafting contracts for transactions, whether such attorneys and paralegals are practicing in the private sector, either as solo practitioners or in law firms, or are employed by enterprise legal departments.

"In this variation, a practitioner would pass, i.e., upload, a draft contract either of his or her own creation, or as drafted by an opposing practitioner (i.e., the test data), to the algorithm. The algorithm would score the entire contract text as against the vector space created by the training documents. The output would be a score for accuracy as to any language in the contract that may be an ambiguity drafting flaw, when the score compares to a high degree with the positive training data for that drafting risk.

"With such an identification of the flaw, a user would access an appropriate appellate court database, e.g., via Google Scholar, and search for and then read the case(s) with the exact or similar phrases, and then decide how best to remedy the flaw.

"While the invention herein disclosed has been described by means of specific embodiments and applications thereof, numerous modifications and variations could be made thereto by those skilled in the art without departing from the scope of the invention set forth in the claims."

Consider the Opposite Purpose

My fourth patent is No. 9,754,218, also issued on September 12, 2017. Let's begin.

"One or more embodiments of the present invention may be deployed for the opposite purpose. In the description above, the experiments pertained to a specific type of risk to be prevented and involved the corporate legal department. However, as the other side of the same coin, the same system can be deployed to surface evidence that would provide support for a financial advantage and provide notice to appropriate employees of the enterprise for confirmation or rejection.

"As such, the system need not be installed in and operated by the legal department and instead would be the province of the Chief Financial Officer or the departments which concern themselves with accounting, tax, or financial matters.

"For example, in major industries such as energy, oil and gas, and telecommunications, companies generate a plethora of documents with unstructured text which may or may not support a Research and Development (R&D) tax credit. A tax credit would reduce the enterprise taxes and preserve net profit, just as avoiding the expense of a lawsuit would.

"However, in order to discern which of these documents support an R&D tax credit and which of those documents are not supportive, a sorting process is, in current practice, undertaken manually. In each instance, the cost is, like litigation, enormous.

"To achieve greater accuracy at a reduced cost, the same system described herein may be trained with documents that were manually sorted in the past, e.g., in one or more previous years, and for each company in any specific commercial sector of endeavor.

"For each sector and a previous manual sorting process, some documents have been identified as positive support for, or as being related to, a financial advantage. Again, as an example, one particular financial advantage is the sought-after R&D tax credit. The documents supportive of claiming an R&D tax credit constitute a positive training set. The documents which are not supportive may also be useful, however, because they generally identify a classification of documents that are unrelated to an R&D tax credit. Such documents constitute a negative set of training documents.

"As a result, and as with the litigation risk example, a binary set of training documents is available. With such documents, the Deep Learning algorithm(s) in the system may be trained to make a binary choice, namely to score the current set of documents that have not been sorted. The documents with high scores according to the algorithm(s), which are related to the positive training set, may be output and displayed to a user in various ways.

"By using appropriate visualization methods such as bar charts and spreadsheets, a user can make use of the true positives to identify a potential financial advantage to be realized.

"While the invention herein disclosed has been described by means of specific embodiments and applications thereof, numerous modifications and variations could be made thereto by those skilled in the art without departing from the scope of the invention set forth in the claims."

I hope you're getting my point. I'm using my life and subject matter experience to explain these variations. Hold off on thinking about the deep learning applications that may be occurring to you. Make notes, but please keep reading.

Stories

Let's begin.

"As yet another variation of the invention, consider the entertainment industry. An enormous problem in the industry is the cost of producing fictional entertainment in the form of books, feature films, television, and other media. However, the benefits can also be enormous for stories that are sometimes first rejected but then become so successful that they become, in their own right, entertainment franchises.

"As a result of success after repeated rejections, a problem has surfaced. The problem is that many thousands of writers and other proponents of allegedly meaningful stories present their work for consideration only to find their works rejected by gatekeepers who supposedly 'know' which proposals will be commercially viable and which of them will fail. Of course, their views are subjective and often wrong.

"This problem of success after repeated rejections has been identified. A partial list of the authors who were repeatedly rejected by publishers include Agatha Christie (rejections for 5 years), J. K. Rowling (12 publishing rejections), Louis L'Amour (200 rejections before first publication), Dr. Seuss, and, among others, Zane Grey.

"And, as for films, there are at least eight (8) films that were rejected before a studio bought the script and wound up with either a major hit or, better still, a franchise: *Pulp Fiction* (1994); *E. T. The Extraterrestial* (1982); *Back to the Future* (1985); *Star Wars* (1977); *Twilight* (2008); *The Exorcist* (1973); *Dumb and Dumber* (1994); and *Boogie Nights* (1997).

"This problem, phrased differently, is this: is there an objective way to assess whether an entertainment proposal will attract an audience large enough to be commercially viable?

"The present invention solves this problem.

"The system enables users to use classified text in a particular context. More specifically, the system begins by amassing an amount of training data from a particular category of text in order to train a Deep Learning algorithm. In this case, however, the corporate legal department may play a role only after a decision has been made to go forward with a book or movie project.

"In this variation, the entertainment categories are well known but have been unappreciated by practitioners in the broad field of artificial intelligence. These categories are called genres.

Such genres are known as, for example, dramas, comedies, and science fiction. There are 18 genres and many fan-transcribed movie and televisions scripts, classified by genre.

"From the above sources (and others) of classified text, in either book or script form, two training sets may be created. For example, a 'positive' training set may consist of commercially successful books or film scripts, while a 'negative' training set may consist of unrelated text such as Wikipedia articles.

"Moreover, it is clear that impactful stories may have structure, as Kurt Vonnegut showed. Using a blackboard, Vonnegut demonstrated that a structure may be depicted over time, with 'good fortune' on the positive portion of the y-axis and 'ill fortune' on the negative portion of the vertical y-axis, and with time on the horizontal x-axis. Following Vonnegut, at least one Deep Learning practitioner has been able to closely approximate Vonnegut's shapes and the shapes of Disney stories as well.

"But while the graphic trajectories of stories may be helpful to decision-makers, the point here is to use classified text and Deep Learning algorithms to bring words and sentiments into focus.

"Once trained, the strength of a Deep Learning algorithm may be assessed and visualized using such techniques as Barnes Hut t-Stochastic Neighbor Embedding, and by the Receiver Operating Characteristic (ROC) curve and the Area Under the Curve (AUC), phrases which are typically combined and referred to as ROC-AUC.

"For humans, words are the carriers of emotions. The system of this invention is capable of learning which assemblages of words and sentiments provide output scores more reflective of commercially viable entertainment projects than otherwise. High output scores may be persuasive to entertainment decision-makers, as they constitute an additional, arguably more objective way to assess the potential for a project *before* substantial costs are incurred.

"Accordingly, this invention calls for a user to select a category and, of the material a user has the right to use, either by copyright or because the material is in the public domain, or otherwise, aggregate the most commercially successful material in digital form and then train a Deep Learning algorithm with that material.

"To clarify, the training data consists of the genre as the 'label,' or classification, and the positive set within each genre consists of the material judged by the marketplace to be the most commercially viable. The negative set would consist of unrelated examples from Wikipedia, or some other dataset, and may include the books or film scripts that resulted in substantial commercial losses.

"Next, this now-classified text would be passed to a Deep Learning algorithm for processing. Once the algorithms' computations are made, each genre-specific algorithm will be in a position to score material it has never before seen, i.e., the material for new projects as they are initially proposed, and as they may be changed and be more fully developed over time by the editing process. Having 'learned' what material within a genre has been commercially viable, the system may provide the publishing and entertainment industries with an additional way to better decide which new proposals and projects *may* be viable, and so enable them to better decide how to allocate their resources.

"In other words, the system will help industry executives avoid the risk of spending enormous sums of money on costly mistakes that could have been avoided.

"As a result, with differently trained algorithms, the submissions of the hopeful creators of new material may be evaluated not only subjectively by humans skilled in the entertainment arts, but also by the more objective system of this invention.

"While the invention herein disclosed has been described by means of specific embodiments and applications thereof, numerous modifications and variations could be made thereto by those skilled in the art without departing from the scope of the invention set forth in the claims."

Medical

The "medical risk" patent is No. 9,754,220, and it's the last of the five patents that were issued on September 5, 2017.

Let's begin.

"One such variation directs the above-described system to the problem of a missed or mistaken diagnosis, which is an outcome not unlike litigation in that a missed or mistaken diagnosis is an adverse and potentially lethal situation. This problem translates into not realizing that specific tests could be ordered to confirm or reject a diagnosis which the healthcare provider has not made but which is indicated by the patient's electronic health records (EHRs), including but not limited to the provider's notes, procedures, medications, tests and test results, pathology reports, and/or diagnostic codes, all of which are collectively hereinafter referred to as Notes. Here, a healthcare provider refers to any professional licensed to provide healthcare services and may include but is not limited to physicians, nurse practitioners, nurses and chiropractors.

"In this variation, a corporate (hospital) legal department may be part of the workflow but is not central to it.

"Nevertheless, this variation involves using the same or substantially similar software system to identify a particular medical risk and provide early warning to healthcare providers. So stated, this variation is entirely different from recent academic papers wherein Deep Learning is trained to make diagnoses or predictions, as if in competition with healthcare providers rather than as an aid to them. See Lipton et al., Learning to Diagnose with LSTM Recurrent Neural Networks (published as a conference paper), arXiv:1511.03677v6 [cs.LG] 1 Mar 2016; and Choi, et al., Doctor AI: Predicting Clinical Events via Recurrent Neural Networks, Proceedings of Machine Learning for Healthcare, arXiv:1511.05942v11 [cs.LG] 28 Sep 2016.

"Briefly stated, the system would be trained by accessing a multiplicity of previous Notes for specific diagnoses, e.g., multiple sclerosis or lupus, where a diagnosis is established by the provider using all the information available in the Notes.

"The training data consisting of a sufficient number (e.g., multiple) of EHRs for each specific *diagnosis* would be gathered up from now-closed cases, which have been made de-identifiable in the sense of being HIPAA ('Health Insurance Portability and

Accountability Act') compliant, e.g., where patient names, among other personally identifiable information, have been redacted before the data is passed to the algorithm. A Deep Learning algorithm would be trained for each specific disease by 'word embeddings' such as word2vec or GloVe, both of which were previously noted.

"For each diagnosis, the provider-made EHRs (in the now-closed, anonymous examples pertaining to a specific diagnosis) would constitute the training set of documents. These documents would be passed, i.e., uploaded, to the algorithm in order to train it. There would be a trained algorithm for each specific disease, as if it were a specific disease risk filter.

"After training, including testing and tuning, the system would ingest provider-made EHRs (e.g., Notes) in open, pending cases, in near real-time or perhaps overnight or in batches for specific blocks of time (e.g., weekly). The system would pass the Notes as data to the algorithms, each of which would evaluate (i.e., score) the Notes, and, when an accuracy score exceeds a user-variable threshold, send its score as an alert to that patient's healthcare provider.

"The alert would also include a specification of what disease or diagnosis is indicated by the physician's Notes, as scored by the algorithm, and may also include a list of symptoms, physical exam findings, tests and/or procedures the provider should consider ordering so that the physician may confirm or deny the diagnosis indicated by the algorithm. As is evident, the alert ignores whether the provider has or has not made a diagnosis.

"In summary, in this variation, the system functions to provide the early warning of a specific medical risk—the risk of a missed or incorrect diagnosis—and so helps to prevent the expense and harm associated with tests, procedures, therapies, or other interventions that may not be germane while also augmenting the physician's ability to avoid an adverse outcome for the patient."

Blockchain

The next description is my eighth patent. Where's the seventh? Since the text of the seventh was the same as the text of the first, and only the claims were different, I've skipped it.

For this "blockchain" patent, I have one introductory comment. This variation uses blockchain to solve the problem of a high value use case but where the amount of data for training purposes is small. In a nutshell, I used blockchain *to enable* deep learning.

The Patent No. is 10,095,992, which was issued on October 9, 2018. It's the first patent issued by the USPTO that uses the terms "blockchain" *and* "deep learning" in a patent's Claims.

Let's begin.

"In the context of text and supervised learning, a Deep Learning algorithm needs a label, category, or classification, along with a training set of examples ('Classified Examples'). The unsolved problem is that of a set of Classified Examples that is small.

"How large must the number of Classified Examples be to adequately train a Deep Learning model of the indicated classification? In the early experiments, a Deep Learning model of the invention successfully identified an instance of discrimination risk in Enron e-mails after training a model with only 50 Classified Examples. This was possible even though MetaMind consultants had suggested that the minimum number of Classified Examples needed to train a Deep Learning algorithm was 200 examples. Hence, getting positive results using only 50 Classified Examples was unexpected.

"Moreover, it is generally understood that, when it comes to Classified Examples as training data, the more the better.

"Thus, one or more embodiments of the present invention addresses the 'small training set' problem. That is, when the training dataset of publicly available Classified Examples is small, i.e., a number substantially less than 200. In such case, a Deep Learning algorithm engaging in supervised learning will likely have an insufficient number of Classified Examples for the algorithm to function with an acceptable level of accuracy.

"But what if an enterprise owns or has access to a 'small training set' obtained as the result of one or more Classified Examples of risks that were settled prior to litigation (such as low-value but high frequency risks, such as employment discrimination disputes, or high-value but infrequent risks such as class actions) or internal investigations into specific risks, such as potential violations of the Foreign Corrupt Practices Act (FCPA), that never became public? Why not combine that data with similar data owned by *other enterprises* facing the same risk? In current practice, to our knowledge, such combinations of enterprises have not been tried. At least one reason for this lack of cooperation is that no single enterprise is likely to want any other (and possibly competing) enterprise, much less a regulatory authority, to see the internal and private data which pertains to a potentially adverse risk situation (hereinafter a 'Situation').

"'Adverse risk' includes losses, such as monetary losses, e.g., fines, penalties, verdicts, or orders for disgorgement; damage to brand or product reputations; legal and associated costs amounting potentially to many tens of millions of dollars.

"Losses may also include diminution of health, e.g., 'zebras' which are rare but adverse health diagnosis (Zebras). See e.g., U.S. Patent No. 9,754,220, titled 'Using classified text and deep learning algorithms to identify medical risk and provide early warning,' to Brestoff et al., which is herein incorporated by reference. Thus, the term Situation should be understood to include Zebras. In that case, where Classified Examples consist of the positive data for the symptoms, tests, and diagnoses which are owned by the patients themselves for each Zebra, the data (and negative data) may be crowd-sourced into a variation of the system described herein.

"As for risks to an enterprise, a few examples will make clear that there are many Situations to address. A potential violation of the FCPA is a clear example of one such Situation. For example, Alcoa's penalty of $384 million in 2014 only ranked it in 10th position. On November 16, 2017, according to an article in *Corporate Counsel*, Wal-Mart reserved $283 million as a *probable* loss, but noted that, in previous filings, the company had reported, for the cost of previous internal investigation, global compliance reforms, and ensuing shareholder lawsuits, a total of about $870 million.

"Other examples are (1) the potential loss of one or more trade secrets, because, by definition, the loss of almost anything marked as 'secret' would be considered as both significant and adverse; and (2) a potential product liability lawsuit or class action.

"One or more embodiments of the present invention addresses the 'small training set' problem.

"As illustrated in FIG. 6, each enterprise ('Owner') identifies training data, i.e., Classified Examples, consisting of a specific situation risk, extracts and stores the data internally (step 602). At step 604, the training data is then processed using a Word Embedding Tool, e.g., GloVe. Word Embedding Tools, such as GloVe, recognizes and skips named entities (that is, words beginning with capital letters, such as company names, individual names, locations, and product names) in creation of the number string.

"Hence, each Owner, as the owner of the data, can turn them into number strings by using a Word Embedding Tool with the same or similar capability, i.e., where named entities are skipped. The result is a small set of Classified Examples, in number string format, for each Situation.

"Thus, as an initial step to ensure privacy, at step 604, each Owner uses the Word Embedding Tool to convert the words that describe an internal investigation into Situation number strings, i.e., Word Embeddings, and does so while the words remain behind the enterprise's firewall. Thus, the entire process 600 is off-chain. The data an Owner would input to the blockchain consists only of the Word Embeddings derived from the data. However, given that a Word Embedding Tool such as GloVe is a publicly available resource with an open lookup table, these number strings need further obscuring.

"So, even though each participating Owner stands to benefit from the results of the future aggregation of its data with the data from other Owners, and the Deep Learning models that may be built from them, each Owner's data (i.e., number strings) must be kept private and obscured from not only the other Owners but also the entity building the Deep Learning model for a given Situation (herein the 'Modeler'). While these and other goals may be achieved contractually, the system and the technology must achieve these goals as well.

"Now two issues arise. The first issue is cheating. Each Owner must be blocked from inputting data that is *unrelated* in some significant way from a given Situation. Neither the Modeler nor any other Owner would benefit from having any Owner pretend that it is submitting data that is related to a Classified Example when it is instead *un*related. Cheating would unjustly reward a cheating Owner as well as diminish the accuracy of the aggregated data and the Deep Learning model built from that data.

"Instead of a technical solution, then, we assume that each Owner behaves rationally for the following reason: If the resulting Deep Learning model is weakened, the 'cheating' Owner who relies on it also will be harmed.

"Thus, the 'verification' aspect of this system requires each Owner to enter into the same contract obligating every Owner to provide data related to the given Situation (as opposed to *unrelated*), where the data consists of communications and documents surfaced by the Owner which are *related to the Situation*.

"This contract would also bar any Owner from either being the Modeler or colluding with the Modeler to attempt to reverse engineer any of the data input by any of the other Owners.

"Alternatively, in the event a contract proves unsatisfactory, verification may be accomplished by contracting with a trusted third party such as a professor of law who is knowledgeable as to the Situation and is at least familiar with neural network and blockchain technologies.

"Thus, each Owner's input will consist of the Word Embeddings converted (at step 604) from its Classified Examples using the Word Embedding Tool, e.g., GloVe, plus an agreed-upon shared secret number (described below as the 'Consensus Number') which is also unknown to the Modeler (step 606). Each Owner inputs its data to the blockchain using a shared private key (the 'Input Private Key') (at step 608). Contractually and otherwise, the Modeler is not given access to (a) the words of any Owner's Classified Examples or the related Word Embeddings, (b) the shared Consensus Number or (c) the shared Input Private Key.

"The output will be the aggregation of all the Word Embeddings of all the Owners, as illustrated in FIG. 7.

"As indicated in FIG. 6, and while each Owner's data remains behind its own firewall, each Owner communicates with the other Owners to form a consensus as to a single number that is not shared with the Modeler, but which is known by each of the Owners (i.e., the Consensus Number).

"Each Owner adds the Consensus Number to its own Word Embeddings (step 606) before using the Input Private Key to upload the Owner's data to the blockchain (step 608). This Input Private Key would not allow an Owner to receive the blockchain's output.

"The second issue is that the Modeler, who receives the block-chain output, which is the aggregate of each Owner's data, must be blocked from reverse engineering any Owner's Word Embeddings.

"To avoid reverse engineering by the Modeler, the system con-templates a contractual provision permitting the Modeler to not only build the blockchain but also a private key the Modeler can use to obtain the output of the aggregated Owner data. This key is the Output Private Key. This Output Private Key would not per-mit the Modeler to provide any input to the blockchain, and the contract would bar the Modeler from sharing the Output Private Key with any Owner.

"Thus, the Modeler does not know the Consensus Number shared amongst the Owners, or the Input Private Key used by the Owners to input their Word Embeddings to the blockchain. The Modeler knows nothing about any Owner's data except for the aggregated result which the Modeler can obtain using the Output Private Key. The Modeler's lack of knowledge concerning each Owner's number strings will make it nearly (if not entirely) impossible for the Modeler to reverse engineer any Owner's input back to the original text.

"On the other hand, the Owners know that the Output Pri-vate Key the Modeler uses to receive output from the blockchain does not enable the Modeler to gain access to any Owner's input to the blockchain.

"It is now appropriate to describe specific examples of the highly adverse Situations this system is intended to address. For example, consider the threat posed by a violation of the FCPA.

If an FCPA violation is the Situation, the publicly available Classified Examples may come from the databases operated by governmental agencies such as the Department of Justice (DOJ) for FCPA. According to Southern Illinois University Law Professor Mike Koehler, a well-recognized expert in FCPA matters, the number of unique FCPA actions available for public review is, since 1977, only about 75.

"Trade secrets are another example of a Situation. The Brooklyn Law School houses a Trade Secrets Institute, but the number of trade secrets ('TS') complaints is also sparse. As of November 17, 2017, the dataset consists of only 86 complaints.

"Product liability is a third example of a Situation. Examples of 'dangerous documents' are scarce, however, for at least four reasons: (1) product liability consultants generally advise that companies train their employees to write e-mails and other documents in a careful manner, in part so as to avoid writing e-mails that clearly express 'safety v. profit' risks; (2) corporate attorneys occasionally (and inappropriately) offer 'word rugs' to employees so that, e.g., instead of saying 'defect or defective,' the employees are advised to say 'does not meet specifications;' (3) defense counsel in product liability cases cannot, without client permission, disclose the 'dangerous documents' they know about; and (4) by regulation, the Consumer Product Safety Commission, after it collects 'dangerous documents' during an investigation, cannot disclose them to the public without the company's consent. See e.g., U.S. Patent No. 9,754,219, titled 'Using classified text and deep learning algorithms to identify entertainment risk and provide early warning,' to Brestoff et al., which is herein incorporated by reference.

"In each of these Situations, companies—and their insurance carriers—would benefit from being able to deploy a Deep Learning model that would provide them with an early warning of the risks, so that corporate counsel could investigate them, and either avoid or mitigate the damages.

"In these and similar Situations, the Modeler will find that the factual allegations from the publicly available, but small, datasets are likely inadequate to build a robust Deep Learning model.

Such publicly available data may, however, be used as a hold-out set for testing and tuning purposes. Alternatively, such publicly available data may be used to improve the accuracy of the Situation model the Modeler develops after receiving the blockchain output.

"FIG. 7 is an illustration of the 'on-chain' process of creating the training dataset for the Deep Learning algorithms. As illustrated, the Word Embeddings 600 from all the Owners (e.g., Enterprises A thru N) are aggregated using a secure multi-party computation (SMPC). In an SMPC, mutually distrusting Owners cooperatively make computations using their still-private data. In the blockchain, the computation is a simple addition or aggregation of each Owner's Word Embeddings (step 702). That is, data from Owner 'A' is added to the data provided by Owner 'B.' The result is added to the data provided by Owner 'C.' The result is added to the data provided by the next Owner and the next. And so on.

"After the Owner Word Embeddings are aggregated, the blockchain will be able to output the resulting aggregation to the Modeler, who will use the Output Private Key to obtain it (step 704). The Modeler will then use that training data 700 to build a Situation model ('Model'), as illustrated in FIG. 1.

"As previously noted, the Model can be tested and tuned by accessing the publicly available data, e.g., the sparse datasets for FCPA and TS categories. In addition, the Model can be tested by a willing Owner in one or more pilot studies. Eventually, a tested Model will be provided to the Owners by the Modeler for deployment within their respective enterprises in accordance with the Consortium contract with the Modeler. Similarly, the Modeler may offer a Model to businesses that are not part of the Consortium, and then the Modeler and the Consortium will share in those revenues.

"In addition, the system provides for both positive and negative feedback loops. For example, an Owner may conduct additional internal investigations for a recurring Situation and input the associated (and additional) training data to the blockchain using the Input Private Key.

"And, after deployment, an Owner may pass its internal enterprise communications through the Model and see that the Model reports a small fraction of the results as 'related' to the Situation, and to what degree. Owner personnel, when reviewing such results, may find that some of the results are true positives and warrant the opening of an internal investigation. Some of the results will be false positives. Owner-specific true positives and false positives, whether from publicly available text in filed lawsuits or from private internal investigations, may be flagged over time, and aggregated, such that the data may be sufficient for a company-specific variation of the Model. This variation would not involve the other Owners.

"Also, in the Owner-Modeler contract, or by amendment to it, the system could be re-configured to permit the inclusion of new Owners.

"The system of this invention contemplates that each multi-party group of Owners is organized by the Modeler and may be viewed as a Situation 'Consortium.' However, the system would function in the same way if one or more Owners formed a Consortium and engaged a Modeler. Notably, the Modeler is a member of the Consortium primarily for the purposes of providing the resulting Situation-specific Deep Learning Models to the Members on such terms as may be set by contract, and to market the Models to non-Members on such terms as may be commercially viable.

"Since the contractual and business provisions governing a Consortium are not pertinent to the operation of the system, they will not be discussed.

"However, it now appears that there is one significant business reason for an Owner to join a Consortium, and not cheat the others. When the system described above is deployed and operated in good faith, it may protect not only each Owner but also the individuals comprising each Owner's decision-makers from criminal actions against them by regulatory authorities such as the U.S. Department of Justice. The reason the system may provide such protection is that its deployment and good faith operation stands as evidence of a specific intent to *avoid* harm, which undercuts any contention of a specific intent to *do* harm. Since there is currently no such thing as a 'compliance defense,' the deployment and 'good faith' operation of the system described herein for early warning may be the best available defense to any accusations of wrong-doing.

"Finally, the scope of this invention is not meant to exclude Convolutional Neural Networks (CNNs). Typically, when we think about CNNs, computer vision comes to mind. After all, CNNs were used in the major breakthroughs involving image classification, e.g., for use by self-driving cars, and other applications for automated photo tagging. In that instance, the problem of small training sets is very well appreciated. However, unless barred by the nation's antitrust laws, the preventive nature of this invention could apply to images as well, especially in the realm of machines engaged in manufacturing a product. In this context, instead of avoiding risk, the system may increase the efficacy of 'preventive maintenance' procedures and operations.

"As an example, consider the problem of property or injury-causing accidents caused by self-driving cars. By design, the CNNs therein are trained with large datasets of video which, among other things, are intended to minimize if not avoid accidents. Accordingly, property and injury-causing accidents are intended to be rare and to occur only occasionally. Video examples may be few and far between, and the same 'small training set' issue may arise. However, for example, the manufacturers of self-driving cars may have, when aggregated, a sufficiently large dataset for analyzing the images leading up and just prior to the accident itself. Accordingly, they may wish to form a Consortium and use the system of this invention as well.

"While the invention herein disclosed has been described by means of specific embodiments and applications thereof, numerous modifications and variations could be made thereto by those skilled in the art without departing from the scope of the invention set forth in the claims."

CHAPTER 8

Post-Litigation

The application for the "blockchain" patent recounted in the previous chapter was filed on January 8, 2018. It was issued on October 9, 2018. That's 25 months after I filed my first patent application on September 27, 2016. It's proof that realizations have no timetable. In this instance, my realization was that I had developed tunnel vision. By this, I mean that I was focusing too narrowly on the concept of deep learning and software systems that would enable "prevention."

But I had known that even a deep learning "early warning" system would never achieve perfection and that business enterprises would be sued. There would be litigation. It was inevitable.

In March of 2019, I realized that there was a post-litigation application. I filed the following application on March 27, 2019. If the USPTO allows it and it issues as a patent, it'll be yet another "continuation-in-part" of my first patent, No. 9,552,548. Please add this: On July 18, 2019, this application was published by the USPTO and assigned U.S. Publication No. 2019-0220937-A1. With this step by the USPTO, I was able to see that my Petition to Make Special had been granted yet again and that the application had been assigned to an examiner.

As before, let's begin.

"In one or more embodiments of the present invention, the context changes to a time when a lawsuit complaint has been filed and served and has come to the attention of an enterprise defendant, whether commercial or governmental. Now the enterprise must engage in a host of e-Discovery processes. One of the earliest of these processes is Early Case Assessment. The purpose is to assess the significance of the lawsuit.

"Prior to doing so, however, the enterprise must understand the lawsuit's nature and which of its personnel (employees or otherwise) might possess documents, for example, e-mails, attachments and other, stand-alone documents such as memoranda or reports, that are potentially relevant to the lawsuit's allegations. As such, they may be custodians of potentially relevant evidence which must be preserved for further analysis. For such personnel, the enterprise must provide such custodians with 'litigation hold notices.' Such notices are designed to avoid spoliation of documents that may be potentially relevant to the matter as well as to enable the enterprise to collect and aggregate the potentially relevant documents. Eventually, such collections will enable the enterprise to comply with future requests by the opposing party for the discovery of electronically stored information (ESI).

"In a standard discovery workflow, the aggregation of potentially relevant documents provides the enterprise with a corpus that may be examined for an early warning of whether the complaint poses a serious or insignificant threat of high costs or other damages, for example, to brand or personal reputations in addition to defense attorney fees, a large settlement or verdict, and, in the worst case, future adverse actions by regulators or the filing of criminal charges by prosecutors. This early examination process is called ECA.

"ECA is a post-litigation process that would use embodiments of the present invention, especially if a deep learning model has already been built for the particular litigation risk described by the complaint.

"Accordingly, instead of focusing on the set of yesterday's e-mails in order to find a risk, for example, of a specific type of litigation, the post-litigation variation would focus each model on the corpus of ESI collected from the custodians of the potentially relevant ESI.

"In addition, if the enterprise has had previous experience with a specific 'nature of suit,' the feedback loop may be different. Before a risk-specific model addresses the newly collected corpus of ESI, the model may be re-trained on the documents that were tagged in previous collections as positive for that specific type of litigation.

"And, after the system scores the newly assembled corpus of ESI, the documents assessed by users as True and False Positives may be used to re-train the model yet again.

"In one or more embodiments, after the model is trained, the system is employed to score the documents in the corpus of ESI.

"The system then identifies documents from that corpus of ESI which are related to the nature of the lawsuit. The identified documents may be flagged to users in the legal department for ECA purposes, for example. The users may then tag, save, and assess the True Positives for case management purposes.

"And both True Positives and False Positives may be saved and used for company-specific retraining of the model when a new lawsuit of the same case-type is filed against the enterprise in the future."

Post-Merger

Claim 1 of my General Risk patents, No. 9,552,548 and No. 9,760,850, pertains to "internal electronic communications," a phrase that includes e-mails but is broader. Similarly, although the Specification pertains to the risk of litigation, the language of Claim 1 addresses "threats or risks of interest." In addition, claim 1 is not time-limited to a *pre-litigation* early warning. For these reasons, these patents may be extended to cover a transaction context: a due diligence aspect of a "merger and acquisition" (M & A) deal. Accordingly, I plan to file an application for yet another continuation-in-part. If allowed, the patent family will grow to 10.

For this example, I won't be quoting from an application. But this variation involves a shift in time *and* perspective, and I hope those shifts will be an eye-opener for your future thinking.

Suppose we're on the buyer's side of a merger or acquisition. In a typical merger agreement, there's a specific amount of time *after* the acquisition for the buyer to request a price adjustment.

But during this post-acquisition timeframe, the buyer has just gained access to and control of the seller's information systems and knows at least some if not all of the names of the members of the due diligence team on the *seller's* side, *and* the timeframe starting with a Letter of Intent and after which the proposed sale was being discussed.

With this information, the buyer can create a corpus of potentially relevant evidence from the names of the members of the seller's due diligence team and, with e-mail threading, the names of the seller's other employees (with a focus on executives) who were in e-mail contact with the seller's team from and after the buy-sell agreement was reached.

Now, what are we looking for? We're looking for assets that have been played "up" and liabilities that have been played "down." Essentially, such conversations border on misrepresentations, deceit, and fraud.

But, if you're the buyer, those are the conversations you'd want your post-closing due diligence team to surface. Can they do that just because they have access to the seller's information archives? No. But can they narrow the search down to a specific corpus? Yes.

Then what? Well, they process the text in that corpus through a deep learning model that's based on deceitful misrepresentations of assets and liabilities or through a deep learning model for the standard litigation category for fraud, which is Nature of Suit code 370.

Next, the buyer catalogs the true-positive conversations and demands a price reduction.

The reason the argument is so persuasive is that, as everyone knows, it's hard to argue with yourself.

CHAPTER 9

Capstone

It's time to revisit what I've written previously, but in a more succinct and more technical way, which will also let me take you on a deeper dive.

For me, the problem was litigation. The solution consisted of deep learning models for text can be used as part of a software system to identify litigation *risks* in enterprise e-mail messages. In short, the solution was an early warning system to enable prevention. The system provides alerts of risky e-mails in near real-time to corporate (in-house) counsel. With alerts, in-house counsel could investigate further and confer with decision makers on ways to address the legal risks before they are realized as lawsuits.

The example here is employment discrimination, a classification of litigation in the U.S. federal court system. With training data for employment discrimination, a deep learning model was built and tested using three different sources of deep learning models: MetaMind, Indico Data Systems, and TensorFlow. ROC-AUC and t-SNE techniques were used to assess each model's accuracy.

The test data consisted of e-mail messages in the Enron dataset. Although Enron was known for fraud, the system surfaced four e-mail messages that were True Positives for discrimination. In employment discrimination litigation, like many other business-relevant classifications of litigation, there is a large amount of training data. But for situations where there is only a small amount of training data, this chapter describes a new approach: the formation of a corporate legal data consortium, and the use of blockchain to perform a secure multi-party computation (MPC). With this technique, a deep learning modeler can build a model for a high-value risk, such as a potential violation of the Foreign Corrupt Practices Act, from the aggregate of consortium data.

In 2008, Professor Richard Susskind, of Oxford University, urged lawyers to warn their clients about impending risks instead of managing litigation.[1] In enterprises, personnel with legal training generally work in corporate law departments. These in-house legal professionals are potentially privy to possible risks contained in internal documents, including but not limited to e-mails and the documents attached to them (hereinafter, e-mails or test data). As the matter stood, they could only manage the litigation caseload and never saw the risks in time to nip them in the bud. The reason is clear: the daily batches of corporate e-mail are too voluminous for in-house counsel to timely and adequately review.

Yet corporate litigation risk is pervasive and can impact the global economy, so the value of being able to discern risks in near real-time is also clear. A system that enables in-house counsel to mitigate or avoid litigation reduces or avoids costly damages: payouts for settlements and verdicts; attorney fees; discovery costs; expert fees; productivity losses; and the potential for diminutions of brand value and personal reputations. In the United States, the average annual cost of commercial tort litigation during the period 2001–2010, in terms of settlements and verdicts, defense fees, and administrative costs, was $160 billion; and that cost, when divided by the average federal and state caseload for the same period, was between $350,000 and $408,000 per lawsuit. The annual savings of avoiding only one lawsuit per month would range between $4.2 million and almost $4.9 million.[2]

The current approach to mitigating or avoiding litigation relies in part on post-litigation seminars and on hotlines for whistleblowers. As for hotlines, they will be used to a greater extent only when an enterprise is willing to encourage their use, and enterprises should do so. A recent study has found that the more employees use hotlines, the less likely the enterprise will face litigation and attendant costs.[3]

Nevertheless, the efficacy of hotlines depends in large part on whether employees use them and how frequently they report to corporate executives or stakeholders. Hotlines are not new, however, and with increasing awareness of the power of Artificial Intelligence, the legal profession now appears to be more willing to try it. For example, in response to a survey in which thousands of attendees of meetings of the Global Pound Conference were asked how dispute resolution can be improved, the top choice of six alternatives, by a significant margin, was "Pre-dispute or pre-escalation processes to prevent disputes."[4]

This chapter describes a software system that operates in a way that is very different from hotlines. The system trains a deep learning model with text extracted from complaints in lawsuits filed in the U.S. federal court system, where each lawsuit is filed in a specific classification or label of litigation risk. The labeled text is used to train a deep learning model for each classification of risk.

When deployed, the system ingests copies of all e-mails that an enterprise generates daily, indexes them, processes them overnight, and scores them to the extent that they relate to the model. The next day, the system outputs only the related e-mails to the personnel in the corporate law department previously designated to receive and assess the results.

If a user deems a result a True Positive, the system allows the user to access the e-mail of interest in its native format. The user may then initiate an internal investigation, conduct e-mail threading (to identify others who may be involved), research internal databases for additional information, and report to a control group executive, who is someone who can make decisions in the name of the enterprise and stands in its shoes.

Since a deep learning model is capable of learning not only from generic examples but also from examples of True Positives that are surfaced when the system is deployed, True Positives can be saved and used to re-train the system. Over time, the model will "learn" and better reflect the culture of the enterprise.

To protect employee privacy, the system would monitor only enterprise computer resources subject to written privacy policies known to and accepted by employees. In connection with e-mail messaging systems, U.S. courts have held that, when such policies are in place, employees have no reasonable expectation of privacy, even when using enterprise systems to communicate with a personal attorney.[5]

A certain number of labeled examples of appropriate text are required to train a deep learning model. Those examples may be found in the U.S. federal court litigation database known as Public Access to Court Electronic Records (PACER).[6] Fortunately, the PACER database is organized into litigation classifications and there is a unique Nature of Suit (NOS) code associated with each classification. In order to initiate a lawsuit in federal court, every person must concurrently complete, sign, and file a Civil Cover Sheet. Along with a complaint, the attorney filing the complaint must review the classifications in the Civil Cover Sheet and comply with the instruction to "Place an 'X' in One Box Only." Accordingly, each lawsuit is mapped to one and only one classification and its associated NOS code.

PACER is a ready source for examples of text typical of each classification and may be searched by specifying only the NOS code. The search will surface case numbers which are active links to the lawsuits filed in that classification. By opening a case link, every document filed in connection with that lawsuit may be accessed.

The first document that tells the story of the risk is the complaint. In PACER, the complaint is usually the first document in the silo of each lawsuit. The facts alleged in each complaint express the filing attorney's factual basis for asserting that the lawsuit has merit. These facts are the essence of litigation risk.

A deep learning model is binary in nature, so that the system will store, score, and report only the e-mails that match up as being "positive," that is, are related to a risk. The system will ignore the other e-mails. Thus, the model must be infused with examples of text that is "positive" and "negative" for the risk.

Generally, the complaints filed in each classification contain generic examples of text that are "positive" for that type of litigation risk. The positive training data may also be shaped by adding examples that are more specific to the enterprise. Such examples may be found by using the NOS code and adding the party name to the search.

To create a generic positive training set for Civil Rights: Employment (NOS 442), that is, employment discrimination, the factual allegations in complaints filed in that classification were extracted from PACER. To create a negative training set, more than 40,000 news articles unrelated to the employment discrimination classification were used.

The next step involved creating a numerical structure for each word in the positive and negative datasets. These numerical structures may be called vectors or number strings. The process of converting words into number strings is generally referred to as a "word embedding." The modern technology for transforming text into number strings was invented in 2013 as word2vec.[7] Word2vec was extended in 2014 by "Glove: Global vectors for word representation," and is referred to as GloVe.[8] With

GloVe, a deep learning model may "learn" English. Here the Wikipedia 2014 + Gigaword 5 corpus was used. It contains six billion total tokens with a vocabulary of 400,000 words. Each vector has a length of 300.

The significance of a word embedding tool is that it converts each word in the same classification of documents into a number string (vector) that a computer can process. This approach implements a key insight by the late linguist J. R. Firth. His now-famous observation is that "You shall only know a word by the company it keeps."[9]

To create a deep learning model for each risk, the number strings are passed to a bi-directional multi-layer Gated Recurrent Unit-based Recurrent Neural Network (RNN). RNNs process sequential information and have "memory" from previous computations.[10]

To assess a model's performance, practitioners typically construct a Receiver Operating Characteristic (ROC) curve and calculate the Area Under the Curve (AUC). The ROC curve plots True Positives on the y-axis with a maximum of 1.0, and False Positives on the x-axis, also with a maximum of 1.0. This space is a 1.0 by 1.0 square such that the maximum AUC score is also 1.0. An AUC score in the eighties or nineties, for example, 0.91, indicates that there are many more True Positives than False.[11]

In addition, data science practitioners often visualize a model by using t-Distributed Stochastic Neighbor Embedding ("t-SNE").[12] A t-SNE visualization shows whether a decision boundary is well-defined between the text related to the risk (the "positive" dataset) and text unrelated to the risk (the "negative" dataset).[13]

The next step is to switch from text in PACER (generic and company-specific) to enterprise text, meaning copies of e-mails obtained from a customized cloud environment, hosted Exchange or Office 365. Such test data may consist of the batch of e-mails that an enterprise generated *yesterday*. Then, each e-mail message is associated with a unique identification (ID) number using dtSearch software.[14] A text file is then passed to a GPU where processing using GloVe and the now pre-trained deep learning model takes place. The result is a file with ID numbers and e-mails that have been scored as being "related" to the risk. That file populates a User Interface (UI) as shown below in Figure 9.1.

Before the UI is presented to a user, the system uses software from dtSearch to access a database containing the words that were initially

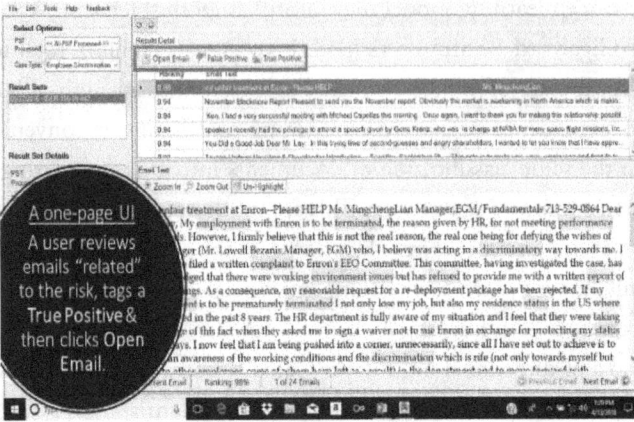

Figure 9.1 **A user interface with scored text and subject matter words (highlighted)**

drawn from the positive dataset in one column and, in another column, only the words that are designated by subject matter experts, that is, experienced litigators, as being relevant to the discrimination risk. Software from dtSearch may be used to access the column with the relevant words and highlight them in UI as a visualization aid for the user.

As Figure 9.1 shows (top rectangle), a user is tasked with making a judgment call and identifying True Positives and False Positives. In addition, a user may also mark/tag an e-mail as True Positive. That tagging places a copy of that e-mail into a database which may be used for re-training the deep learning model at a future date. After deciding that an e-mail is a True Positive, a user can also view that e-mail in its native format and export it to a case management system. Finally, with a True Positive result, an internal investigation may begin.

Besides this functionality, the system is designed to keep the output confidential and limited to the in-house attorney and the client enterprise. It does this by taking advantage of two confidentiality rules: the work-product doctrine and the attorney-client privilege.

For the work-product doctrine to apply, the system must be deployed by members of the corporate law department (or other enterprise personnel under the direction and control of the law department) and then used as defined: "in anticipation of litigation." The work-product doctrine should also apply when a law department employee concludes that an e-mail is a True Positive, retrieves that e-mail in its native format, and then conducts an internal investigation to determine whether the litigation risk is supported by other information.

If the investigation supports a conclusion that a risk exists and that damages may ensue (or have only recently be incurred), enterprise law department personnel may contact a control group executive, to advise that person of the matter and what may be done about it. Now the attorney-client privilege should apply.

Now for results. An early version of the above-described system was evaluated by two different deep learning providers. They each were given the same positive and negative training data, and the same "test data," a portion of Enron e-mails from the inbox of Ken Lay, former Chairman and CEO of Enron.

However, before these evaluations, the PACER database was reviewed for statistics about Enron. For the five-year period 1997–2001, the chance of finding an employment discrimination case against an Enron company was very small. During that five-year timeframe, Enron was a named party in PACER 1,339 times. However, Enron was a named party in only 13 employment discrimination lawsuits, which amounts to only about one percent (1 percent).

The first evaluation was conducted with a deep learning system provided by MetaMind, a startup founded by Richard Socher, one of the authors of the GloVe paper. Given the training data described above, the MetaMind model was asked to assess approximately 5,000 Enron e-mails by Ken Lay, who had not been directly involved with the Human Resources department. Using MetaMind's model, the amount of training data was increased in baby steps. The experiment involved only 50 positive training examples at first. It was re-run with 100, 150, 200, and finally 400 examples.

Surprisingly, the MetaMind model trained with only 50 examples produced immediate results. The result was a set of 24 e-mails (out of about 5,000, a fraction of about one-half of one percent) that were scored as being "related" to the risk. In reviewing the top-scoring e-mails, the data showed that while most of the e-mails were False Positives, one was a True Positive. The result was doubly surprising as Enron was known for fraud, not employment discrimination.

Later, the Enron test set was expanded to include other Enron employees, where three e-mails scored almost as high as the first. However, each e-mail presented the same risk, because they were "forwards" of the e-mail first sent to Ken Lay.

Each of these e-mails included the phrase "my unfair treatment at Enron" and read in part as follows:

> [M]y employment with Enron *is to be terminated, the* reason given by HR, for not meeting performance standards. However, I firmly believe that this is not the real reason, the real one being for defying the wishes of my manager . . . , who, I believe was acting in a discriminatory way towards me (Italics added; in the UI, only "terminated" was highlighted.)

In this e-mail, the word "terminated" drew attention to the words that preceded it: "is to be," common words which were not relevant, but which provided important context. "Is to be terminated" indicated that no job action had yet been taken. And since no other damages had been identified, the e-mail appeared to have been written before damages could be alleged. Because damages are a necessary element of every civil lawsuit, a user would infer that a lawsuit was not yet viable. Thus, the deep learning model had surfaced an e-mail that signaled a potential lawsuit.

Further experiments with a list of sex and race terms added little to the strength of the model. These lists of key words lacked context and were as potentially misleading to users as any list of keywords, a finding first made in 1985.[15]

The first evaluation ended when MetaMind was acquired in March of 2016 by Salesforce.com. MetaMind was closed in April.

Based on further research, Indico Data Systems, Inc. ("Indico") was approached and became the second testbed. Indico's deep learning model was trained with the same training data sourced from PACER and the same test data that came from Enron. The Indico model surfaced the same risky e-mail as the MetaMind model, the one regarding "My unfair treatment at Enron." That e-mail, which scored 0.86 and 0.88 with MetaMind, received a comparable score from Indico's model: 0.89.

Then, without being asked to do so, Indico used approximately 75 held-out documents and created a ROC graph with a calculation for the AUC. In an e-mail, Dan Kuster, a data scientist at Indico, reported that the AUC score was 0.967, a high score, and commented that "the classifier is strong."[16]

At this point, and rather than continue with Indico, an open-source option was chosen. In November of 2015, prior to these experiments, Google announced the availability of an open-source version of TensorFlow. With TensorFlow, even in its earliest 1.0 version, the results were substantially similar or better.

The next step was a confidential trial with an enterprise listed on the NYSE. After in-house counsel successfully tested the system with Enron e-mails, a production set of e-mails was uploaded from a now-closed employment discrimination case. This batch of e-mails was new to the system, and the results were mixed. The system succeeding in surfacing at least one e-mail that was known to in-house counsel, and at least one e-mail that was previously *unknown* and which in-house counsel reported was "material." But the trial ended when the system's overall accuracy was deemed insufficient to assess the company's production of two million e-mails per month.

After the trial ended, the challenge was addressed. The "negative" text was combined with 10,000+ Enron *e-mails* that were curated to avoid the e-mails previously determined to be related to employment discrimination. The model had previously learned English. Now it was learning English in the context of e-mails. The ROC-AUC score went even higher, from 0.967 to 0.997.

The re-trained deep learning model was then presented with a held-out set of 20,401 Enron e-mails. Re-trained, the system surfaced 25 e-mails related to the risk, a fraction equal to 0.00122, which is about one-eighth of one percent. The 4x improvement was significant. See the t-SNE depiction in Chapter 4 (Figure 4.3).

As you know, a weak model will have some positive training documents in the negative cluster and perhaps some negative documents in the positive cluster. A strong model will not suffer from this "mixing." With fine-tuning, the "end game" is a t-SNE visualization indicating that the decision-boundary between the positive and negative clusters is free of this confusion. In the context of the training data I was using, I attributed the clear decision boundary to the fact that the quality of the training data was high. I was using attorney-vetted text related to the discrimination risk.

Now the previous "accuracy" objection could be addressed.

A human reviewer might well suggest that the task of finding four True Positives in 20,401 e-mails (a small fraction equal to 0.000196) during a single day is impossible (or with a large team, very expensive), but that finding four True Positives in a set of only 25 related e-mails (a much larger fraction which equates to 4/25 or 16 percent) is possible. But now assume that the system must be able to process two million e-mails *per month*, as posited by in-house counsel at the NYSE company. Divide 2,000,000 e-mails by 4.3 weeks per month: the result is 465,116 e-mails *per week*. Then divide 465,116 e-mails per week by 5 days per week: the result is 93,023 e-mails *per day*. But then, applying the "accuracy" fraction of 25/20,410 = 0.00122, the result is that a TensorFlow model, trained as described, would surface for human review only about 112 e-mails related to the discrimination risk *per day*. In 2015, the average number of business e-mails a user sent and received per day was 122; and is expected to grow by the end of 2019 to 126 messages per day.[17]

Combined, three conclusions may be drawn: (1) the savings due to a prevention technology is likely very substantial; (2) the pattern-matching ability of a well-trained deep learning model is a viable filter which enables users to "predict" future lawsuits; and (3) the size of the law department team may be estimated from the amount of enterprise e-mails per month and may result in a high return on investment.

As noted, PACER is a U.S litigation database of nationwide scope. In the context of "civil" litigation (distinct from appellate, bankruptcy, and criminal litigation), there are many business-relevant classifications, for example, insurance, breach of contract, healthcare, fraud, and civil rights-employment. In these categories, there were over a thousand complaints filed in 2018.[18] The model-building process for each such PACER classification would be built in the same way as the employment discrimination example described above.

However, a fundamental and previously unsolved problem arises when the amount of data available to train a viable deep learning model is small. While the problem is general, this chapter describes a solution in the context of a specific litigation risk.

For example, consider the matter of a potential violation of the Foreign Corrupt Practices Act (the FCPA). There is no such PACER classification, but it is a high-value, adverse risk to any U.S. enterprise doing business in other countries. An FCPA violation may include monetary losses, for example, fines, penalties, verdicts, or orders for disgorgement of more than $1 billion[19]; imprisonment for as long as 180 months[20]; and let's not forget any damage to company and personal reputations.

The data available to train a deep learning model for FCPA violations is small. From 1977 to 2004, complaints with factual allegations in pleadings were used to file cases but less than 80 complaints were made public. From 2004 to the present, the pleadings have been replaced by non-prosecution agreements, deferred prosecution agreements, administrative orders, or declinations with disgorgements.[21]

This chapter now describes how blockchain technology can be used to address and solve the small training data problem. The first issue is privacy. In connection with such high-value litigation risks, enterprises do not share the data they gathered in their own internal investigations for the understandable reasons that no enterprise wants competitors or regulatory authorities to know about its potential FCPA violation.

To address this privacy concern and yet solve the "small training data" problem, a Corporate Legal *Data* Consortium can be formed. Each consortium would be governed by a formal joint venture agreement focused on addressing the risk of the same adverse situation.

In such a joint venture, there is one general partner, the deep learning "Modeler." The limited partners are enterprises that are concerned about potential violations of the FCPA and have relevant data to share.

While the consortium partners would owe fiduciary duties to each other by agreement, including the risk of non-disclosure of the training data that each limited partner would provide, that "glue" is probably insufficient. To ensure that each limited partner's data is not disclosed to anyone else, each consortium would use blockchain to enable the creation of a deep learning model.

First, each limited partner would identify its own internal training data consisting of, for example, a capstone memo and/or supporting e-mails related to its previous internal FCPA investigations. The text in these documents would then be processed with GloVe to convert the words of these documents into number strings. In contrast to the previous description for building a deep learning model from publicly available text, here the conversion of words into number strings would take place while the documents, and the words in them, remain behind the enterprise's firewall.

In addition, each limited partner would add an agreed-upon shared secret number, a "Consensus Number," to the number strings for the documents it intends to put "on chain." By agreement, the Consensus Number would not be revealed to the Modeler.

Then each limited partner would use an Input Private Key to upload its number strings to an appropriate provider of blockchain for the legal industry, for example, Integra Ledger[22] or a blockchain firm that's already performing secure MPCs for business use cases, for example, Sharemind.[23] The limited partners would have the only Input Keys but would not possess an Output Private Key. On the other hand, the Modeler would have no Input Key and would possess the only Output Key.

Once the training data is on-chain, a secure MPC would be performed for the purpose of aggregating the number strings contributed by each limited partner. The Modeler receives only the aggregation, not the ingredients. Since the Modeler receives the aggregation of the data, the Modeler may then overcome the problem of a training set that is otherwise too small.

Before a model may be useful, however, it must be validated. Once a deep learning model for a specific situation has been created, the Modeler would provide it to the limited partners who may they validate it by testing it on the documents in their own previous investigations, including investigations that were not used as inputs. Each limited partner would then describe to the other partners how the model performed. The process would be iterated until the members of the joint venture were satisfied with the model's efficacy.

Once a model is validated, the limited partners would use it in accordance with the terms of the joint venture agreement. Then, on such terms as the agreement would provide, the joint venture can offer the model to other enterprises that are *not* part of the consortium. The consortium partners would share in the resulting revenues in accordance with their joint venture agreement.

This use of blockchain *to enable* the construction of a deep learning model is likely to require a significant up-front commitment. But it has the potential to enable the creation of a deep learning model where the amount of training data is small but the value of preventing a risk is high.

The blockchain solution to the "small training dataset" problem is a roadmap for future work in general. In the litigation context, future work will include implementations, testing, and evaluation of potential FCPA violations and at least two other litigation contexts.

Notes

1. Susskind (2008).
2. Brestoff and Inmon (2015).
3. Stubben and Welch (2018).
4. Barton and Groton (2018).
5. *Scott v. Beth Israel Med. Ctr.*, 17 Misc. 934, 847 N.Y.S.2d 436 (2007); and *Holmes v. Petrovich Development, LLC*, 191 Cal.App.4th 1047, 119 Cal. Rptr.3d 878 (2011). January 12, 2019. https://scholar.google.com/
6. PACER (2019).
7. Mikolov, Sutskever, Chen, Corrado, and Dean (2013).
8. Pennington, Socher, and Manning (2014).
9. Wikipedia (2018).
10. Young, Hazarika, Poria, and Cambria (2018).
11. Wikipedia (2019).
12. Maaten and Hinton (2008).
13. Linderman and Steinerberger (2017).
14. dtSearch (2018).
15. Blair and Maron (1985).
16. Kuster (2016).
17. The Radicati Group, Inc (2018).
18. United States Courts (2018).
19. Richard (2018).
20. Jessica (2016).
21. Koehler (2018).
22. Integra (2018).
23. Sharemind (2018).

CHAPTER 10

First Dots

Remember Connect the Dots, a game for children? How about BMEWS, the acronym for the Ballistic Missile Early Warning System, a billion-dollar Cold War strategy? Do you recall the criticism leveled at the CIA and the FBI after the September 11 attack in 2001? Did you know that the U.S. Center for Disease Control and Prevention has had a program since 2014 to prevent various forms of violence? In the first training session I watched, I finally learned the point of its program: it's the First Dot that matters.

Let me explain.

In the game that many have played, and which we still present to children, a cluster of dots forms some pattern that isn't recognizable until the dots are connected. The dots may be numbered or lettered, and kids learn to start with "1" or "A" and go from there to "2" or "B." For a link at a collection of over 50 of these games (free and last updated on October 5, 2018), see the endnote.[1]

But in 1958, BMEWS was an acronym for finding a First Dot. It was a radar, computer, and software system that was built between 1958 and 1961 as a strategy to give our military a 15 to 25-minute early warning of an intercontinental ballistic missile attack by the Soviet Union. The Wikipedia link to BMEWS (last updated on October 2, 2018) is the second endnote.[2]

The First Dots, of course, would have been the detection of missiles coming at us from over the horizon.

Now fast forward to September 11, 2001. I was in Los Angeles and awake early. I turned on the TV to see the news was one of the Towers in New York had been hit by a jet and was on fire. My wife Lois was traveling to San Diego and I called her. While I was on the phone with her, I saw the second plane fly into the other Tower. Lois stopped to go into a diner. The TV was on but wasn't tuned to a news channel. She knew what others didn't.

I learned from her that it's mentally difficult to know about a First Dot and know that it's true when others don't have a clue.

But 9/11 wasn't the First Dot. Although the CIA and FBI were criticized for not sharing their respective stores of data and connecting the dots, the problem was opaque because the First Dot didn't come with a number or a letter. It had to be tracked down and evidently wasn't apparent until the plot's organizer, Ramzi Yousef, was arrested. With enough puzzle pieces, the story could be re-assembled.

And for a step-by-step of the dots that led to 9/11, and how they were connected, see the PBS's *Frontline* episode, "Connecting the Dots." According to this look in the rear-view mirror, 9/11 had its genesis with the World Trade Center attack … in 1993.

If you're curious, here's the link to the PBS *Frontline* webpage and the "Connecting the Dots" episode. The site that allows you to take a step-by-step tour through the dots is a PBS webpage.[3]

Now, more recently, the U.S. Center for Disease Control and Prevention has developed a training program to teach the public how to recognize the links between multiple forms of violence. The first training session begins in the same way I started this article—with the game that children play.[4]

Evidently launched in October of 2014, the Veto Violence trainings address the violence due to child abuse and neglect, intimate partner violence, sexual violence, suicide, and youth violence.[5]

From this video, it dawned on me that the First Dot was critically important for risk detection *and avoidance.*

But what if the First Dot is a *false alarm?* Well, history shows us that even our missile defense systems can suffer from false alarms. Had we not found their causes within a matter of minutes, the disaster could have been catastrophic on a *global* scale.

For this topic, see the *New York Times* article—*Causes of False Missile Alerts: The Sun, the Moon and a 46-Cent Chip* (January 13, 2018).[6]

Now let me translate. When an artificial intelligence (AI) model for a specific risk reports a high-scoring e-mail as being "related" to the risk, and corporate counsel reads that e-mail and assesses it as being a True Positive, that e-mail is a candidate for further consideration as a First Dot … and only then will anyone authorize an internal investigation.

But what if there is no early recognition of a First Dot and so no early warning? That's entirely possible. My point is this: Without AI as way for a human being to recognize a potential First Dot, there's no reason for anyone to even try to sift through the cluster of yesterday's e-mails to find the risky ones.

Ah, but what about whistleblowers and hotlines?

The good and bad of hotlines are that companies sometimes have them but don't encourage their use. And, while some employees may use hotlines, many may not use them for fear of reprisals (as in "kill the messenger").

Are they the best we can do? No. And, in my view, AI disrupts them.

Are you trying to find First Dots? Probably not.

But that's what motivated me to go for a patented deep learning system. The software we created takes your company's e-mails *from yesterday*, scores them against a previously identified pattern for a specific risk, and provides a user with candidates for an internal investigation. Then, after that investigation, a user could hope to learn whether one of those high-scoring e-mails was the First Dot.

To Know or Not to Know

At this point,[7] I address a question that more than one person has asked: "Wouldn't the attorneys, or the executives, prefer *not* to know?"

Or this variation on that theme: "What if the enterprise knew and didn't do anything? If the failure to act, after having knowledge, were to be discovered, wouldn't that be worse than not knowing about the threat in the first place?"

So we must be clear-eyed about this. Our view is this:

[T]he profession needs to rethink its role from that of an ambulance at the *bottom* of a cliff (remedial practice) to helping people to manage risks on top of the cliff. While the practice at the bottom of the cliff can be very profitable, clients and consumers should be reminded to avoid practices that are detrimental in the longer run.

To practise [sic] preventive law, we must first work with relevant data. Some of our colleagues may not consider this part of the job description of the legal function, but it is down to us to embrace it or watch someone else do so in the course of taking our profession to the next level. In today's big data era, this is not an option, but a *necessity*.[8]

But do *attorneys* perceive any need to change? Historically, the answer is no. As the Hon. John Facciola (U.S. Magistrate Judge, retired) has recounted, "the telephone was in existence for 10 years before lawyers started to use it. They thought it was beneath their dignity."[9]

So, there are obstacles, and we can list some of them. First, we face the momentum in the legal profession which argues against change, especially when the change involves technology. While some of the lawyers who are litigators must now learn to understand technology in the e-discovery aspects of every lawsuit, they still resist it. Yet many litigators do not know how to use that necessary but admittedly specialized technology.

In fact, they are not even proficient with the basics, such as software programs for word processing, spreadsheets, and PDFs. And this is why D. Casey Flaherty, formerly in-house counsel at Kia Motors America, and Suffolk University's School of Law recently launched the Suffolk/Flaherty Legal Tech Audit.[10]

In July of 2013, Flaherty explained:

My hypothesis is that lawyers in general are woefully deficient in using the software tools at their disposal—for example, Word, Acrobat, Excel. To test this, I provided associates at outside firms with mock assignments. Sample tasks include (a) formatting a motion in Word, (b) preparing motion exhibits in PDF, and (c) creating an arbitration exhibit index in Excel.

I've administered the audit 10 times to nine firms (one firm took it twice)… *[A]ll the firms failed—some more spectacularly than others. The* audit takes me 30 minutes… Both the median and mean (average) pace rounded to five hours.[11]

Second, we face the momentum that has in-house counsel acting as procurement and matter managers of the cases in which an enterprise is involved. They depend on the "bench" of outside law firms to do the heavy lifting.

Third, in-house counsel may balk at having a tool which permits them to take on the mantles of investigator and analyst. Is this the practice of law? Can't the IT or HR departments do this work instead of us?

Fourth, in-house counsel may resist a change which permits them to be strategic business partners with the company's other leaders. Who's in charge?

Fifth, the larger *plaintiff-oriented* law firms may resist any change that reduces the number of prospective plaintiffs. Their reason for being is to redress harm and to recover damages. With fewer deaths, injuries, and other civil wrongs, there would be fewer prospective plaintiffs, and the plaintiffs' "bar" would have fewer clients to represent. (However, they can hardly complain if their stated goal is achieved, but in some other way. Who can wish for more deaths, injuries, and other civil wrongs?)

Sixth, the larger *defense-oriented* law firms may resist any change that reduces the number of lawsuits for them to defend. Their firm revenues are based, in part, on the number of cases they are engaged to defend, and the number of hours they bill to defend them. They have no financial interest in seeing these metrics go down.

And, any early warning system, at least in its early versions, may produce a number of false positives, such that early adopters may look for an early exit and return to their comfort zones.

Finally, it could turn out that many business leaders might genuinely prefer to simply deal with lawsuits as they come, to be strictly customer-facing, and to stick with driving revenue and profits.

It seems that there are many reasons "not to know."

But I contend that humans have learned, in other contexts, that it is far better to know than not to know. The Greeks knew this long ago: *Forewarned is forearmed.* The ostrich defense—sticking one's head in the sand to avoid knowing about a nearby predator—has never worked very well for the ostrich. In American jurisprudence, this defense is not known as being a successful strategy, and has been alternatively called the dumb CEO defense, dummy defense, idiot defense, or Sergeant Schultz defense.[12]

In my view, it is better to suffer through some number of false positives than to be blind-sided by a preventable litigation catastrophe.

I think Bill Gates would agree. In 1999, he wrote a book, Business @ the Speed of Thought,[13] to which he devoted a whole section and six chapters to explain his perspective. For example, Chapter 10 was entitled, "Bad News Must Travel Fast." He even went a step further, and began the section this way:

> I have a natural instinct for hunting down grim news. If it's out there, I want to know about it. The people who work for me have figured this out. Sometimes I get an e-mail that begins, "in keeping with the dictum that *bad news should travel faster than good news,* here's a gem…."[14]

Gates provides lots of examples, including from the computer industry. He mentioned IBM, when its mainframe and minicomputer businesses were undermined by the PC; Digital Equipment Corporation, when its minicomputer business was undercut by still smaller PCs, which DEC had dismissed as toys; and Wang, which lost the word processing market when it stuck with putting word processing software on dedicated hardware systems rather than on the PC.[15]

He also mentions Ford, Douglas Aircraft, and why the United States was not prepared for the attack on Pearl Harbor.[16]

Gates advised this:

> A change in corporate attitude, encouraging and listening to bad news, has to come from the top…The bearer of bad tidings should be rewarded, not punished…You can't turn off the alarm and go back to sleep. Not if you want your company to survive….[17]

Gates asserts that leaders should heed the early warnings from salespeople, product developers, and customers, *but he doesn't mention the Legal Department.* We can excuse the Legal Departments of the past. They had no way to see litigation in-the-making, and so could not sound off to give what Gates called an "alert."

But now they *can* see. An alert from a system intended to prevent litigation is like a smoke alarm: When it goes off, it doesn't necessarily tell you there's a fire; but you have to pay attention to it.

Notes

1. Fisher (2019).
2. "Ballistic Missile Early Warning System" (2019).
3. Frontline (2002).
4. CDC (Centers for Disease Control and Prevention) (2017).
5. Ibid. https://vetoviolence.cdc.gov/apps.connecting-the-dots/node/4/ (first of seven training videos) (accessed June 14, 2019).
6. Stevens and Mele (2018).
7. The original source of this blog article is Chapter 24 of *Preventing Litigation: An Early Warning System to Get Big Value Out of Big Data* (Business Expert Press 2015). My use of the material here is permitted by my contract with the publisher. My Intraspexion colleague, Larry W. Bridgesmith, added the points concerning the criminal sentencing guidelines and Sarbanes Oxley.
8. Tung (2015).
9. Hon. John Facciola (2015).
10. Flaherty and Perlman (2015).
11. Flaherty (2013).
12. U.S. Legal, Inc (2015).
13. (Bill) Gates and Hemingway (1999).
14. Ibid. at 159–60.
15. Ibid. at 179–80.
16. Ibid. at 180. For the Pearl Harbor example, Gates cites Gordon Prange, *At Dawn We Slept* (New York: McGraw Hill, 1981) at 439–92 (chapters 54 through 59), for communications breakdowns and "fundamental disbelief" on the U.S. side during the weekend of December 6–7, 1941.
17. Ibid. at 179.

CHAPTER 11

The Future

In a previous chapter, I recounted having attended an event in Seattle put on by the United States Chamber of Commerce. It was jointly presented by the Institute for Legal Reform and the Center for Emerging Technologies.

One of the speakers said something like "Big Data is the new oil." I made a connection then with AI in the form of deep learning, and I'm repeating it here:

"If Big Data is the new oil, deep learning is the new refinery."

Here's my overview of the ingredients of the New Refinery as follows, asserting that they consisted of the Computer Processing Units (CPUs) + Graphics Processing Units (GPUs) + Deep Learning algorithms (DL) + Applications revealing useful insights (A); that is, CPUs + GPUs + DLs + As.

I also see two other revolutions on the horizon and would like to give you an "early warning" about them.

On the hardware side, I think we must take note of the efforts to develop better hardware, the so-called Quantum Computers.

Quantum Computing (QC) involves a computer that operates in an entirely different way from the computers with which we're familiar. In the world we experience as humans, the physics is a classical approximation of Nature, which is quantum mechanical.

The computers we use today are digital and binary, meaning that they operate in two specific states of either one (1) or zero (0), as if there were only two choices, e.g., "true" or "false" or "yes" or "no." The data encoded in this way are called "bits."

QC uses a quantum processing unit (QPC) and a "superposition" of states called "quantum bits" or "qubits" for short. I won't delve into the development of a QPC except to alert you to the fact that the idea was first proposed in 1980 and has an associated timeline.[1]

In 1981, the late Caltech professor, Richard Feynman, is reported to have said: "Nature isn't classical, dammit, and if you want to make a simulation of nature, you'd better make it quantum mechanical, and by golly it's a wonderful problem, because it doesn't look so easy."[2]

Quantum Computers have been under consideration for nearly 40 years, but the pace of innovation has recently accelerated. In March 2017, IBM announced a QC system with an open Application Programming Interface (API) called (not surprisingly) IBM Q. In less than two years, on January 8, 2019, IBM announced IBM Q System One as the first integrated quantum system for commercial use.[3]

In December 2017, Microsoft announced a preview version of a developer kit with a programming language called Q#.[4] This language is for writing programs that run on an emulated quantum computer. At its Build conference in May 2019, Microsoft announced it would, during the summer of 2019, open-source parts of its Quantum Developer Kit on GitHub, including the Q# compiler and quantum simulators.[5]

Google's in the hunt, too. In March 2018, Google's Quantum AI Lab announced a 72 qubit processor called Bristlecone.[6] And on July 19, 2018, Google announced an open-source framework called Cirq and plans for a Bristlecone cloud.[7] More recently, on February 21, 2019, Google announced a *cryogenic* controller that uses only two miliwatts of power.[8]

But with respect to hardware, has anyone seen the light? Yes. There are three startups—Luminous, Lightelligence, and Lightmatter—who are developing computing chips which, instead of using electrons, are powered by light.[9] Such devices are known as optical processors.

Why are startups working on them? Simple: optical processors using lasers and "waveguides" may be a faster, better way for computers to carry out the ever-increasing number of mathematical calculations that some (but not all) AI applications demands.

And, speaking of demand, recent AI advances are requiring, and getting, an amount of compute power which exhibits a doubling time of just under *four months*.[10]

So the next question is whether the software that would run on quantum computer is being developed. And the answer is yes, that's beginning to appear too.

In January of 2018, a paper by Dernbach, Mohseni-Kabir, Towsley, and Pal was published called Quantum Walk Inspired Neural Networks for Graph-Structured Data. We now have yet another abbreviation: QWNNs.[11]

The first author is Stefan Dernbach. At that time, he was a PhD student at the Computer Networks Research Group at the University of Massachusetts College of Information and Computer Sciences. There are three co-authors: Arman Mohseni-Kabir, Don Towsley, and Siddarth Pal. Towsley was Dernbach's PhD advisor. Mohseni-Kabir was a graduate student in the physics department at UMass Amherst. Pal was a scientist with BBN Raytheon Technologies.

The abstract reads in part:

> We propose quantum walk neural networks (QWNN), a new graph neural network architecture based on quantum random walks, the quantum parallel to classical random walks. A QWNN learns a quantum walk on a graph to construct a diffusion operator which can be applied to a signal on a graph. We demonstrate the use of the network for prediction tasks for graph structured signals.

Note the phrase, "prediction tasks." *That's* what's so promising. Like it or not, we want, and need, AI to help us do in the future what we humans cannot now do. I think we'll be hearing a lot more about Quantum Computers and some variation of QWNN.

Notes

1. Wikipedia (2019).
2. Gil (2016).
3. System One IBM Q (2019).
4. Microsoft (2019).
5. Nguyen (2019).
6. Whitwam (2018).
7. Nott (2018).
8. Wiggers (2019).
9. Giles (2019).
10. Amodei and Hernandez (2018).
11. Dernbach, Mohseni-Kabir, Pal, Towsley, and Gepner (2018).

CHAPTER 12

The Future Is Open

In closing, and in other words, we're in a different ballgame now. We've moved beyond transistors and integrated circuits. The AI revolution, featuring deep learning, has demanded change. And change is going to come, and it will be as to *everything*.

As a business leader, I hope that you've now learned how to work with your data scientist. The future belongs to you. Please invent some of it.

References

"AI and Drones Help Farmers Detect Crop Needs." 2018. *NVIDIA*, https:// news.developer.nvidia.com/ ai-and-drones-help-farmers-detect-crop-needs/ (accessed June 15, 2019).

"AI vs. Lawyers: The Ultimate Showdown." 2018. https://lawgeex.com/resources/ aivslawyer/ (accessed June 3, 2019).

Agrawal A., J. Gans, and A. Goldfarb. 2018. "Cheap Changes Everything." In *Prediction Machines: The Simple Economics of Artificial Intelligence*. Boston: Harvard University Press.

Agrawal A., J. Gans, and A. Goldfarb. 2018. "Your Learning Strategy." In *Prediction Machines: The Simple Economics of Artificial Intelligence*. Boston: Harvard University Press.

Amodei, D., and D. Hernandez. May 16, 2018. "AI and Compute (blog)." *Open AI*, https://openai.com/blog/ai-and-compute/ (accessed June 14, 2019).

(Bill) Gates III, W.H., and C. Hemingway. 1999. *Business @ the Speed of Thought: Using a Digital Nervous System,* 159–200. New York, NY: Warner Books Inc.

"Ballistic Missile Early Warning System." 2019. https://en.wikipedia.org/wiki/ Ballistic_Missile_Early_Warning_System/ (accessed June 14, 2019).

Barton, T.D., and J.P. Groton. 2018. "Forty Years on, Practitioners, Parties, and Scholars Look Ahead—The Votes Are In: Focus On Preventing and Limiting Conflicts." *Dispute Resolution Magazine* (Spring 2018), 9–10. American Bar Association.

Blair, D., and M.E. Maron. 1985. "An Evaluation of Retrieval Effectiveness for a Full-Text Document-Retrieval System." *Communications of the ACM* 28, no. 3, pp. 289–99.

Brestoff, N.E., and W.H. Inmon. 2015. *Preventing Litigation: An Early Warning System to Get Big Value Out of Big Data*. New York, NY: Business Expert Press.

"Chinese Technology Conglomerate Kuang Chi to invest $20 Million in EyeSight Technologies, A Leader in Embedded Computer Vision." 2017. *Eyesight Technologies*, http://eyesight-tech.com/news/chinese-technology-conglomerate-kuang-chi-invest-20-million-eyesight-technologies-leader-embedded.computer-vision/7/ (accessed June 15, 2019).

"Convolutional Neural Network." 2019. *Wikipedia*, https://en.wikipedia.org/ wiki/Convolutional_neural_network/ (accessed June 15, 2019).

CDC (Centers for Disease Control and Prevention). 2017. https://vetoviolence. cdc.gov/apps/connecting-the-dots/ (accessed June 14, 2019)

Church, K. 2007 "A Pendulum Swung Too Far." *Linguistic Issues in Language Technology*. http://languagelog.ldc.upenn.edu/myl/ldc/swung-too-far.pdf/ (accessed June 3, 2019).

Colvin, G. 2016. "The AI Revolution: Why You Need to Learn About Deep Learning." *Fortune*, October 5. http://fortune.com/2016/10/05/ai-artificial-intelligence-deep-learning-employers/ (accessed June 15, 2019).

Cox, J. 2017. "Making Your Client Special." *The Hillsborough County Bar LAWYER*, https://cdn.ymaws.com/www.hillsbar.com/resource/resmgr/magazine/Lawyer_Summer_2017.pdf/ (accessed June 15, 2019).

Dernbach, S., A. Mohseni-Kabir, S. Pal, D. Towsley, and M. Gepner. 2018. "Quantum Walk Inspired Neural Networks for Graph-Structured Data." https://arxiv.org/abs/1801.05417v2/

dtSearch. 2018. "dtSearch Corp." January 12, 2019. http://dtsearch.com/

Fisher, S. 2019. "53 Free Connect the Dots Worksheets." https://thesprucecrafts.com/connect-dots-worksheets-1357606/ (accessed June 15, 2019).

Flaherty, D.C. July, 2013. "Could You Pass this In-House Counsel's Tech Test? If the Answer is No, You May be Losing Business." *ABA Journal*, https://abajournal.com/legalrebels/article/could_you_pass_this_in-house_counsels_tech_test (accessed April 8, 2015).

Flaherty, D.C., and A. Perlman. 2015. "Suffolk/Flaherty Legal Tech Audit." www.legaltechaudit.com (accessed April 8, 2015) ("The test takers will finalize a redlined investors' rights agreement (word processing). They will then be given data on dividend payments to investors to investigate whether payments were made equally to all investors (spreadsheets). Finally, they will prepare an e-filing attaching the agreement and spreadsheet (PDF)").

Fogg, A. 2018. "A History of Deep Learning." *Import.io* (blog). May 30, https://import.io/post/history-of-deep-learning/

Foote, K. 2017. "A Brief History of Deep Learning." *Dataversity* (blog). February 7, https://dataversity.net/brief-history-deep-learning/

Frontline. 2002. "The Man Who Knew." https://pbs.org/wgbh/pages/frontline/shows/knew/etc/connect.html ("Connecting the Dots" Map) (accessed June 14, 2019).

"Eyesight Technologies Closes New China Auto Deal with Hefei Zhixin Automotive." 2019. http://eyesight-tech.com/news/eyesight-technologies-closes-new-china-auto-deal-with-hefei-zhixin-automotive/ (accessed June 15, 2019).

Gil, D. 2016. "The Dawn of Quantum Computing is Upon Us (blog)." https://ibm.com/blogs/think/2016/05/the-quantum-age-of-computing-is-here/ (accessed June 14, 2019).

Giles, M. June 13, 2019. "Bill Gates Just Backed a Chip Startup that Uses Light to Turbocharge AI." https://technologyreview.com/s/613668/ai-chips-uses-optical-semiconductor-machine-learning/ (accessed June 14, 2019).

Hon. John Facciola (interviewed by Zoe Tillman). April, 2015. "Law at the Speed of Technology." *Corporate Counsel*, p. 56.

"IO View is a Computer vision AI for Rapid Damage Assessment Named After the Native Hawaiian Hawk." 2019. *OceanIT*, http://oceanit.com/products/ioview/ (accessed June 15, 2019).

Ibid. https://vetoviolence.cdc.gov/apps.connecting-the-dots/node/4/ (first of seven training videos) (accessed June 14, 2019).

Integra. 2018. "Integra, Inc." https://integraledger.com/

Jessica, T. 2016. "Jessica Tillipman: The Ten Longest FCPA-Related Prison Sentences." January 12, 2019. http://fcpablog.com/blog/2016/8/15/jessica-tillipman-the-ten-longest-fcpa-related-prison-senten.html

Keel, S., J. Wu, P.Y. Lee, J. Scheetz, and M. He. 2018. "Visualizing Deep Learning Models for the Detection of Referable Diabetic Retinopathy and Glaucoma." *JAMA Ophthalmol* 137, no. 3, 288–292. doi:10.1001/jamaophthalmol.2018.6035

Koehler, M. 2018. [e-mail.].

Kuster, D. 2016. "Intraspexion custom API + results (Confidential)." [e-mail.].

"Latent semantic analysis." 2019. https://en.wikipedia.org/wiki/Latent_semantic_analysis (accessed June 3, 2019).

Lambert, F. 2017. "Tesla has Opened the Floodgates of Autopilot Data Gathering." *Elecktrek*, https://electrek.co/2017/06/14/tesla-autopilot-data-floodgates/ (accessed June 15, 2019).

Lambert, F. 2018. "Tesla Deploys Massive New Autopilot Neural Net in v9, Impressive New Capabilities, Report Says." *Electrek*, https://electrek.co/2018/10/15/tesla-new-autopilot-neural-net-v9/ (accessed June 15, 2019).

Lambert, F. 2018. "Watch a Tesla Drive in Paris through the Eyes of Autopilot." *Electrik*, https://electrek.co/tesla-autopilot-sees-drive-paris/ (accessed June 15, 2019).

Lambert, F. 2019. "Watch Tesla Autopilot Reacting to a Stop Sign and Making a Right Turn." https://electrek.co/2019/05/29/tesla-autopilot-stop-sign-making-turn/ (accessed June 16, 2019).

Linderman, G.C., and S. Steinerberger. 2017. "Clustering with t-SNE, Prov=ably." arXiv:1706:02582. January 12, 2019. https://arxiv.org/abs/1706.02582v1/

Maaten, L.V.D., and G. Hinton. November 2008. "Visualizing Data Using t-SNE (PDF)." *Journal of Machine Learning Research*, no. 9, 2579–05.

McCormick, C. 2019. "Word2Vec Tutorial—The Skip-Gram Model." http://mccormickml.com/2016/04/19/word2vec-tutorial-the-skip-gram-model/ (accessed June 3, 2019).

Microsoft Speech Translator. 2019. https://skype.com/en/features/skype-translator/ (accessed June 3, 2019).

Microsoft. 2019. "Get Started with Quantum Development." https://microsoft.com/en-us/quantum/development-kit/ (accessed June 15, 2019).

Mikolov, T., I. Sutskever, K. Chen, G.S. Corrado, and J. Dean. 2013. "Distributed Representations of Words and Phrases and their Compositionality." In *Advances in Neural Information Processing Systems*, 3111–19. Google Scholar.

Nguyen, C. May 6, 2019. "Quantum Goes Open Source as Microsoft Expands Q# Programming Language." https://digitaltrends.com/computing/microsoft-q-quantum-computing-open-source/ (accessed June 15, 2019).

NOAA (National Oceanic and Atmospheric Administration). 2012. *Lidar 101: An Introduction to Lidar Technology, Data, and Applications*. Washington, DC: NOAA. https://coast.noaa.gov/data/digitalcoast/pdf/lidar-101.pdf (accessed June 15, 2019).

Nott, G. July 19, 2018. "Google Launches Quantum Framework Cirq, Plans Bristlecone Cloud Move." https://computerworld.com.au/article/644051/google-launches-quantum-framework-cirq-plans-bristlecone-cloud-move/ (accessed June 15, 2019).

"Optimize Every Plant." 2019. *Blue River Technology*, https://bluerivertechnology.com/ (accessed June 15, 2019).

"Petroleum Product." 2019. *Wikipedia*, https://en.wikipedia.org/wiki/Petroleum_product/ (accessed June 15, 2019).

PACER. 2019. "Public Access to Court Electronic Records." January 12, 2019. https://pacer.gov/

Parloff, R. 2016. "Why Deep Learning Is Suddenly Changing Your Life." *Fortune*, September 26. http://fortune.com/ai-artificial-intelligence-deep-machine-learning/ (accessed June 15, 2019).

Peccarelli, B. 2019. "The real star of Davos? Artificial intelligence." *Thomson Reuters* (blog). January 31. https://blogs.thomsonreuters.com/answeron/the-real-star-of-davos-artificial-intelligence/ (accessed June 19, 2019).

Pennington, J., R. Socher, and C. Manning. 2014. "GloVe: Global Vectors for Word Representation." https://nlp.stanford.edu/projects/glove/ (accessed June 3, 2019).

Pennington, J., R. Socher, and C. Manning. 2014. "Glove: Global Vectors for Word Representation." In *Proceedings of the 2014 Conference on Empirical Methods in Natural Language Processing (EMNLP)*, 1532–1543. Google Scholar.

Radford, R. 2009. "How to Ford a River." *Washington Trails Assn.* https://wta.org/go-outside/trail-smarts/how-to/how-to-ford-a-river (accessed June 3, 2019).

Rajasekharan, A. 2019. "What are the Main Differences between the Word Embeddings of ELMo, BERT, Word2vec, and GloVe?" (blog), April 15. https://quora.com/What-are-the-main-differences-between-the-word-embeddings-of-ELMo-BERT-Word2vec-and-GloVe/ (accessed June 15).

Richard, L.C. 2018. "Petrobas Smashes the Top Ten List (and We Explain Why)." January 12, 2019. http://fcpablog.com/blog/2018/9/28/petrobras-smashes-the-top-ten-list-and-we-explain-why.html/

Rouse, M. 2018 "Recurrent Neural Networks." https://searchenterpriseai.techtarget.com/definition/recurrent-neural-networks/ (accessed June 3, 2019).

"Short Circuit." 2019. *Wikipedia*, https://en.wikipedia.org/wiki/Short_circuit (accessed June 15, 2019).

"Sources of Photography." 2019. *Google*, https://google.com/streetview/explore/ (accessed June 15, 2019).

"Speech Recognition Breakthrough for the Spoken, Translated Word." 2012 https://youtube.com/watch?v=Nu-nlQqFCKg (accessed June 3, 2019).

Scott v. Beth Israel Med. Ctr., 17 Misc. 934, 847 N.Y.S.2d 436 (2007); and Holmes v. Petrovich Development, LLC, 191 Cal.App.4th 1047, 119 Cal. Rptr.3d 878 (2011). January 12, 2019. https://scholar.google.com/

Sharemind. 2018. "Cybernetica AS." January 12, 2019. https://sharemind.cyber.ee/sharemind-mpc/

Stevens, M., and C. Mele. 2018. "Causes of False Missile Alerts: The Sun, the Moon and a 46-Cent Chip." *The New York Times*, January 13. https://nytimes.com/2018/01/13/us/false-alarm-missile-alerts.html

Stubben, S., and K.T. Welch. 2018. "Evidence on the Use and Efficacy of Internal Whistleblowing Systems." January 12, 2019. http://dx.doi.org/10.2139/ssrn.3273589/ (accessed on December 2018).

Stumpe, M., and C. Mermel. 2018. "Applying Deep Learning to Metastatic Breast Cancer Identification." *Google AI Blog (blog)*, October 12, https://ai.googleblog.com/2018/10/applying-deep-learning-to-metastatic.html/ (accessed June 14, 2019).

Susskind, R.E. 2008. "The End of Lawyers?" *Rethinking the Nature of Legal Services*, 224. Oxford: Oxford University Press, Great Britain.

System One IBM Q. 2019. "Making the World's First Integrated Quantum System." https://research.ibm.com/ibm-q/system-one/ (accessed June 14, 2019).

"Technology." 2019. *Waymo*, https://waymo.com/tech/ (accessed June 15, 2019).

The Radicati Group, Inc. 2018. "E-mail Statistics Report–2015-2019." Retrieved E-mail Statistics Report, 2015-2019 Executive Summary on January 12, 2019. https://radicati.com/?p=12960/

Tung, K. March, 2015. "A Kodak Moment for the Legal Profession." www.lexology.com/library/detail.aspx?g=2eae2fe3-8226-45b2-931e-97b7d66ed7d1/ (accessed April 11, 2015). In 2008, Law Practice Guru Richard Susskind, Who Endorsed *Preventing Litigation*, said as much in *The End of Lawyers? Rethinking the Nature of Legal Services*, 224. Oxford: Oxford University Press.

U.S. Legal, Inc. 2015. "Ostrich Defense Law and Legal Definition." http://definitions.uslegal.com/o/ostrich-defense/ (accessed April 27, 2015). Furthermore, an ostrich defense does not open the door to favorable treatment for being proactive under the criminal sentencing guidelines, and defies the mandates of Sarbanes Oxley requiring publicly traded companies and their executives to adopt and use proactive policies and procedures to uncover fraud and illegality.

United States Courts. 2018. "Table C-2—U.S. District Courts-Civil Federal Judicial Caseload Statistics." Retrieved on January 12, 2019. https://uscourts. gov/statistics/table/c-2/federal-judicial-caseload-statistics/2018/03/31/

Vincent, J. 2017. "Walmart is Using Shelf-Scanning Robots to Audit its Stores." *The Verge*, https://theverge.com/2017/10/27/16556864/walmart-introduces-shelf-scanning-robots/ (accessed June 15, 2019).

"We're building the World's Most Experienced Driver." 2019. *Waymo*, https:// waymo.com/ (accessed June 15, 2019).

"What is Street View." 2019. *Google*, https://google.com/streetview/ (accessed June 15, 2019).

Wadhwa, V. 2011. "The Case for Old Entrepreneurs." *The Washington Post*, December 2. https://washingtonpost.com/national/on-innovations/the-case-for-old-entrepreneurs/2011/12/02/gIQAulJ3KO_story.html?utm_term=. bb4449b29dd2

Walker, E. 2019. "#Squad Goals: How Automated Systems are Helping us Work Smarter." *Walmart*, https://news.walmart.com/2019/04/09/squadgoals-how-automated-assistans-are-helping-us-work-smarter/ (accessed June 15, 2019).

Whitwam, P. March 6, 2018. "Google Announces 'Bristlecone' Quantum Computing Chip." https://extremetech.com/extreme/265105-google-announces-bristlecone-quantum-computing-chip (reviewed on June 14, 2019).

Wiggers, K. February 21, 2019. "Google's New Cryogenic Quantum Controller Uses Less than 2 Milliwatts." https://venturebeat.com/2019/02/21/googles-new-cryogenic-quantum-controller-uses-less-than-2-milliwatts/ (accessed June 15, 2019).

Wikipedia. 2018. "Wikipedia: the Free Encyclopedia." January 12, 2019. https:// en.wikipedia.org/wiki/John_Rupert_Firth/

Wikipedia. 2019. "Quantum Computing." https://en.wikipedia.org/wiki/Quantum_computing/ (accessed June 14, 2019).

Wikipedia. 2019. "Wikipedia: the Free Encyclopedia." January 16, 2019. https:// en.wikipedia.org/wiki/Receiver_operating_characteristic/

Young, T., D. Hazarika, S. Poria, and E. Cambria. 2018. "Recent Trends in Deep Learning Based Natural Language Processing." arXiv:1708.02709.v8 January 12, 2019. https://arxiv.org/abs/1708.02709v8/

About the Author

Nelson E. (Nick) Brestoff, in 2014, when he retired, had over 38 years of litigation experience. He began his career as prosecutor for the City of Los Angeles, and then went to the private sector, switching to civil litigation in both the federal and state courts in California. He held an AV Preeminent Martindale rating (highest possible peer review rating) for many years.

As an attorney, Nick represented both plaintiffs and defendants. His cases included breach of contract, breach of fiduciary duty, civil rights, construction, environmental, employment, fraud, insurance coverage, professional liability, real estate entitlement (zoning), trade secret and patent litigation, and fraud and unfair competition.

His notable "first chair" results were for plaintiffs in *City Solutions, Inc. v. Clear Channel Communications*, 365 F.3d 835 (9th Cir. 2004) (jury trial and appeal; client collected $10.1 million); a shareholder derivative action (confidential; collected $4.4 million); and in *Little v. Auto Stiegler, Inc.* (2003) 29 Cal.4th 1064 (arbitration trial; client collected $742,000).

Beginning in 2010, Nick began writing articles about eDiscovery issues. His work has been published by the World Jurist Association, the American Bar Association, the Organization of Legal Professionals, and by *Law Technology News*.

In 2012, Nick wrote the first article about *electronic* preventive law, "Data Lawyers and Preventive Law" (*Law Technology News*, October 25, 2012).

Nick's education includes a Bachelor of Science degree in Engineering Systems from the University of California at Los Angeles (UCLA), and a Master of Science degree in Environmental Engineering Science from the California Institute of Technology. He received his Juris Doctorate degree from the University of Southern California (USC) Gould School of Law.

In 2015, Nick was the lead author of *Preventing Litigation: An Early Warning System to Get Big Value Out of Big Data* (with W.H. Inmon). Between 2016 and 2018, Nick invented software systems using deep learning and blockchain for which eight patents were issued (in 2017 and 2018) by the United States Patent and Trademark Office.

He lives in Sequim, Washington.

Index

OTHER TITLES IN OUR BUSINESS LAW AND CORPORATE RISK MANAGEMENT COLLECTION

John Wood, Econautics Sustainability Institute, Editor

- *Preventing Litigation: An Early Warning System to Get Big Value out of Big Data* by Nelson E. Brestoff and William H. Inmon
- *Understanding Consumer Bankruptcy: A Guide for Businesses, Managers, and Creditors* by Scott B. Kuperberg
- *The History of Economic Thought: A Concise Treatise for Business, Law, and Public Policy, Volume I: From the Ancients Through Keynes* by Robert Ashford and Stefan Padfield
- *Buyer Beware: The Hidden Cost of Labor in an International Merger and Acquisition* by Elvira Medici and Linda J. Spievack
- *The History of Economic Thought: A Concise Treatise for Business, Law, and Public Policy, Volume II: After Keynes, Through the Great Recession and Beyond* by Robert Ashford and Stefan Padfield
- *European Employment Law: A Brief Guide to the Essential Elements* by Claire-Michelle Smyth
- *Corporate Maturity and the "Authentic Company"* by David Jackman
- *Conversations in Cyberspace* by Giulio D'Agostino

Announcing the Business Expert Press Digital Library

Concise e-books business students need for classroom and research

This book can also be purchased in an e-book collection by your library as

- a one-time purchase,
- that is owned forever,
- allows for simultaneous readers,
- has no restrictions on printing, and
- can be downloaded as PDFs from within the library community.

Our digital library collections are a great solution to beat the rising cost of textbooks. E-books can be loaded into their course management systems or onto students' e-book readers.
The **Business Expert Press** digital libraries are very affordable, with no obligation to buy in future years. For more information, please visit **www.businessexpertpress.com/librarians**. To set up a trial in the United States, please email **sales@businessexpertpress.com**.

www.ingramcontent.com/pod-product-compliance
Lightning Source LLC
Chambersburg PA
CBHW061323220326
41599CB00026B/5011